YELLOW ROSES
ON HER FEET

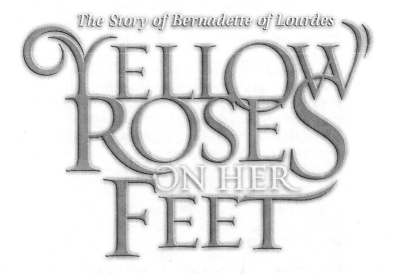

The Story of Bernadette of Lourdes

YELLOW ROSES ON HER FEET

LETITIA M. MORSE

Yellow Roses on Her Feet: A Story of Bernadette of Lourdes by
Letitia M. Morse (1920–)
147 pages, 5x8 inches, 203x127 mm, three appendices.
Library of Congress Control Number: 2008927814
ISBN: 978-0-9815075-0-7

Cover/interior design: Brian Gage, www.briangagedesign.com
Illustrations: Parker Fitzgerald at Brian Gage Design
Map: Michael S. Bezruchka
Interior layout: Michael W. Perry
Lourdes photographs: Brother Lawrence Lew, O.P.

Published by:
Bienna Books, Brier, Washington
United States of America
www.biennabooks.com
Persevere to Sure Victory in Christ

THIS BOOK IS DEDICATED TO

ST. BERNADETTE

AND TO THE

IMMACULATE HEART OF MARY

TABLE OF CONTENTS

A Lady with Yellow Roses on Her Feet

A strong wind blew, but the leaves on the poplar trees were still. "Where is the wind coming from?" thought Bernadette, looking around nervously.

The girl's gaze went upward, toward a radiant light emerging from a cave in the cliff. To her utter amazement, a lovely young woman appeared within the golden glow. Bernadette was enraptured. Never had she seen anyone as beautiful as this Lady.

The exquisite vision bowed and extended her arms to Bernadette. She wore a long white dress, held at the waist by a sky-blue sash. Light yellow roses adorned each of her bare feet. A white veil covered the Lady's head and shoulders and fell the length of her dress, rippling in the slight breeze. She smiled lovingly.

Fourteen-year-old Bernadette Soubirous was the only person who saw this apparition on February 11, 1858, near Lourdes, France. But that moment was to change her life forever, and to transform the town of Lourdes.

The Lady appeared to Bernadette seventeen more times in the next several months. She requested that a church be built at the site. She asked Bernadette to dig with her hands in the mud, and from that place an abundant spring of pure water began to flow. Sick people who bathed in the water were cured.

At each succeeding appearance, some people in Lourdes and the surrounding area became fascinated. Others became scornful and scoffed, "Who does this Bernadette think she is, telling stories about seeing a beautiful Lady that no one else can see? Isn't she the daughter of the poverty-stricken François and Louise Soubirous? Why, she can't read or write. She hasn't even received her First Communion."

While officials and villagers pestered Bernadette and her family with questions and ridicule, hundreds and then thousands of devout pilgrims flocked to the grotto where the Lady appeared. Many were healed of terrible illnesses and their faith revived.

In 1933, the Pope canonized Bernadette as a saint of the Catholic Church, inviting all to accept the heavenly origin of her visions.

Now, more than 150 years later, millions of pilgrims visit the Lourdes shrine every year. A magnificent basilica stands on the site. And people continue to be healed in body and spirit.

Read and admire the story of this obscure young girl whose visions inspired so many people. Saint Bernadette's life is one of gentle courage in the face of terrible poverty, intrusive publicity, and intense physical suffering.

CHAPTER ONE
LIFE AT BOLY MILL

On a windy dawn in late spring of 1854, church bells rang in the bustling market town of Lourdes in southern France. Hot sun soon poured over the foothills of the Pyrenees Mountains into the valley where Bernadette Soubirous lived with her family at Boly Mill. The air was fragrant with roses and alive with the trilling and chirping of birds.

Bernadette and her younger sister, Marie "Toinette" Antoinette, slipped into their blouses and full skirts, and ran outside. They watched horse-drawn carts loaded with sacks of grain ford the millstream below their house. Poor women approached on the footbridge. All were bringing their grain to be ground into flour at the Boly Mill. Bernadette and Toinette were excited because other children were coming to play in their family's big mill yard and splash in the Lapaca Stream running under the mill.

On this Thursday, the cobbled streets echoed with the clopping of horses' hooves and the clatter of wooden shoes—for it was market day in Lourdes. Farmers from the outlying hills drove their carts to town to sell their produce, to shop at the stores and to bring their grain to the mill to be ground into flour.

Horses were used for every kind of job because there were neither trucks nor automobiles in Lourdes. Steamships crossed the ocean and great noisy machines manufactured many kinds of goods in the large cities. But most people in the small town of Lourdes had not seen such things.

Bernadette eagerly watched their family's customers arrive. She also kept an eye on her little brother, Jean-Marie "Johnny," while her parents were busy in the mill. He was fascinated by the jingling bells of the horses. When he got close to their iron-shod hoofs, Bernadette pulled him out of danger.

The older boys jumped out of the carts and waded into the cold, turbulent stream. They balanced on the slippery rocks, while their friends tried to push them off. Johnny begged Bernadette to let him stand on the rocks, but she refused with gentle firmness, "No. It is too dangerous. You might drown." She led him to a grove of trees where the smaller children were shouting and playing.

The farmers' daughters were soon skipping with Bernadette and Toinette, and playing the same games that their mothers had played when they were growing up. Bernadette was ten years old and small for her age. But she was so animated that Toinette and the farm girls looked to her to make the games lively. Her chestnut braids shone in the sunlight and her brown eyes sparkled. She beckoned the shy farm girls to join in the games, making sure that everyone was having fun.

The din of rushing water, the grinding of the great millwheels, and the barking of the dogs almost drowned out the laughter of the children. Men shouted over the noise as they unloaded heavy sacks from their wagons and helped Bernadette's father, François, pour their grain into his mill chute. They watched as the grain flowed down to the big stone wheels that ground it into flour.

The miller enjoyed exchanging news and jokes with his customers, who were also his friends. They knew him well—a shy man, good-natured but independent, an expert miller and a fine hunting companion. François was proud of his small mill and pleased with his young wife, Louise, and their three active children.

Even while playing, Bernadette was watching for the Lagües family to arrive. She had a special bond with Marie Lagües. Marie had nursed Bernadette when she was a baby because her own mother had been too ill to nurse her. Bernadette sometimes visited her foster family at their farm near the hilly village of Bartrès, just three miles away.

When the Lagües arrived, Bernadette rushed to greet Marie and her children. Marie ascended the steps into the big kitchen of the millhouse, holding a baby on one arm and carrying a heavy basket with the other. The sturdy farmwoman was far different from Bernadette's own slender mother. Bernadette followed her foster mother happily, knowing the basket held special treats for her.

While Bernadette placed the oranges and little cakes that Marie had brought for her into her own basket, she noticed her mama drop the Lagües' payment for the milling into a small box. It was the custom for the miller's wife to look after the business affairs of the mill, and to entertain the women customers. Bernadette's mama always invited the ladies to a lunch of wine, cheese and homemade bread, chattering cheerfully as she did so. She refused the coins that poor widows tried to pay, yet she gave them generous portions of the lunch.

Bernadette was hurrying outdoors with her treats when she overheard Marie talking to her mother. "Louise, I am worried about that child. She is too small. She is not growing well."

Glancing back, Bernadette saw a shadow fall over her mama's blue eyes. "I know," Louise agreed. "It's the asthma. She was up again last night, coughing and gasping for breath. We surely will have to keep her home from school again this year. We can't send her out in the cold weather."

Bernadette's cheeks burned. She hated it when people talked about her health. For the fourth year in a row, she would be held back from school. If only her parents understood how much she wanted to read and write, to do sums and to draw. François and Louise had never been to school themselves, and they could not imagine why it was so important to their daughter. They thought the eldest girl in the family ought to learn the skills of crafts and child care, and help her mother.

Bernadette's younger sister, Toinette, and all her friends were already going to school and knew how to write and do arithmetic. They studied the catechism and listened to stories about Jesus, but Bernadette could neither read nor write. She was far behind.

Bernadette was impatient to make her First Communion. She knew that Jesus was already in her heart, but she could not receive him in Holy Communion without learning the catechism—those hard questions and answers about her religion. If she could not go to school again this year, how long would it be?

Shaking off her sadness, Bernadette ran back into the yard to share her treats with the others. After playing in the hot sun, they especially enjoyed the juicy oranges. The people in Lourdes did not often get these golden fruits of Spain.

Spain was not far away; it was just on the other side of the Pyrenees. But those tremendous mountains divided France from Spain and traders avoided crossing them with their goods. Instead, oranges from Spain were transported by ship over the ocean, and then brought up the Gave River in barges to the market at Lourdes.

While the other children continued their play, Bernadette went over to her cousin, Jeanne Védère, who was pushing a young child on the swing. Jeanne was sixteen and Bernadette admired her. The Védère family, who lived several miles away in the city of Tarbes, was quite rich. Jeanne was even allowed to drive her own carriage with a finely bred horse.

Jeanne had just graduated from the convent school in Tarbes and hoped to become a nun as soon as she could get her godmother's permission. Bernadette was impressed by her cousin's flowery dress and chic bonnet, her graceful walk and refined "convent" manners. Most of all, she appreciated her gentle and sweet spirit. It was to Jeanne that Bernadette confided her deep longing to receive Holy Communion. This cousin was the only one who seemed to understand.

Today, however, Bernadette had something else that she was anxious to confide. "Jeanne, please help us," she began. "Mama is so generous that when people pay her, she never counts the money, and if they do not pay, she trusts them to remember next time. But many do not pay her at all.

"When Grandmother lived here, she used to write down how much each one paid, or even how much it was worth if they gave a chicken or some vegetables instead of money. If they did not pay, she reminded them the next time of how much they owed. Mama does not do that, and sometimes she does not have enough money to buy clothes for us. The mill needs repairs, and I know Papa is worried about that."

Bernadette gazed earnestly at her wise older cousin. "You know all about arithmetic, Jeanne. Please teach Mama how to manage the money."

Jeanne blushed. "My dear little one," she exclaimed. "I could not offer to teach your mama. She would be so—oh, so—embarrassed. No, it would not do at all. Not at all," she said, shaking her head vigorously.

"Perhaps you could ask your Aunt Bernarde," Jeanne suggested. "She is used to doing business with her husband, is she not? After all, she is your mama's older sister—she would be the right person to help her."

"Oh, no," exclaimed Bernadette. "Aunt Bernarde has already tried to help, but she makes Mama feel stupid. Mama begins to cry and then Aunt Bernarde goes off in a huff. Aunt Bernarde is too smart and Mama is afraid of her.

"But you are just as clever, Jeanne," she added hastily. "And you are so gentle that I am sure you could help Mama without hurting her feelings. Please do it," she pleaded.

Jeanne took Bernadette's small hand in her own long, slim fingers, and looked at her gravely. "I am afraid it will not do, little one," she answered. "There are some things we just have to trust God for. I am sure He will look after your mama—she is so kind and giving. He will reward her for it someday."

These words comforted Bernadette. When the customers left, she remained outdoors while the shadow of the great castle on the cliff above Lourdes crept over the mill yard. She swung back and forth on the old swing until the evening Angelus bells rang out. While she murmured the familiar words of the prayer, she gazed at the Gave River, glistening red in the setting sun. She knew it flowed out to the great Atlantic Ocean. Across that ocean were lands where people were building new countries. She wondered what it would be like to cross the ocean in a big ship and to see those strange lands.

Little did she dream that one day her name, Bernadette Soubirous, the miller's daughter from the little town of Lourdes, would be flashed by telegraph all across Europe, and her story told in those new lands. But before that time, Bernadette and her family would suffer many hardships.

CHAPTER TWO

THE SOUBIROUS LOSE THEIR HOME

The summer of 1854 was hot and dry. The grass turned brown and the river became low and sluggish. Few customers came to Boly Mill now that the river had lost its power to turn the great wheel of the mill. Bernadette and Toinette were listless and bored. They missed bouncing balls and skipping rope with their playmates. They spent hours in the once tempestuous stream that had now become a shallow brook—safe enough to play in, even for their little brother, Johnny.

It was sad to see Papa pace along the bank of the stream, chewing a piece of grass and frowning. No longer was their home a hive of bustling activity. Mama often sat in silence, gazing mournfully at the cloudless sky; her hands idle in her lap.

Then one day an unexpected visitor came to the mill, a young man named Armand Soubirous, Papa's cousin. The children were excited when he rode towards the house on his white horse. They ran to fetch their Papa.

To Bernadette's surprise, her father strode toward his cousin without a word and stopped him before he could enter the yard. Armand dismounted and the two men stood face to face, talking heatedly.

François became more and more upset as he responded to his cousin and gestured towards his children. Finally, he turned away abruptly and marched stiffly into the house, his face grim and tense. The young man galloped back along the road, his horse's hoofs sending up puffs of dust from the stony track. The children looked at each other fearfully.

They followed their papa into the house. He was kneeling before the crucifix, his head bowed on his hands. Their mama was sobbing. Impulsively Toinette peppered her with questions. "What's wrong with Papa? Why did Armand go away? Is he coming back?"

"Don't cry, Mama," wailed little Johnny, as he hurled himself at his mother and clung to her legs.

Bernadette said nothing, although she felt sick with worry. She had noticed for some time that her parents had very little money. She knew that Armand had bought the mill from their former landlord and guessed that he had come to demand his rent, though Papa could not pay right now. It was not until later that her mama and papa would tell their children the bad news. If they could not pay the rent, they would have to leave the little mill house where Bernadette had been born, and where her mother had grown up.

Through the long, hot months, they struggled to make the rent payments—hoping that torrents of rain would soon fill up the river and set the mill rumbling again. Although little by little they sold almost all their possessions to get money for rent and food, they managed to hang onto the wardrobe cabinet that had been hand-carved by Bernadette's grandfather.

The dry heat lingered on through September and October. While Toinette was at school, Bernadette remained at home. She and her mother mended the few remaining clothes, patched the thin skirts, and darned the worn socks. They chopped carrots and onions for the weak soup that was their usual supper.

They walked with little Johnny along the banks of the stream, gathering twigs and branches to kindle the fire. They sang snatches of old songs and Bernadette coaxed her mama to laugh by doing imitations of their former customers. Her heart ached for her mother, once so vivacious and pretty, but now pale and weary. In spite of Bernadette's efforts to cheer her, Mama often sighed and wiped away tears.

The best times for Bernadette were her rambles in the woods with her father. He tried to pretend that everything was fine, teasing her, and making a game of teaching her the wood lore his own father had taught him.

"See if you can fill your basket with chestnuts before I find five rabbit holes," he would say. Then he pretended to be a hare, hopping on the ground, stopping and peering around as if frightened. At such times, Bernadette laughed heartily.

Bernadette and her papa enjoyed their walks, but their purpose was serious. They had to find food in the forest, for the family had little to eat otherwise. On a good day, they came home with a hare for the soup pot or a brace of wild pigeons for a pie. Often they came home with nothing. Wild animals were scarce in this dry year. Even the trout had almost disappeared from the stream.

One night, Bernadette overheard her parents talking. "I don't understand where all the money went," sighed her papa. "I worked hard. We had many customers. We should have been able to save enough to last until the rain comes again."

"It's my fault," moaned Mama. "I didn't make sure our customers paid for the flour we milled for them. I gave away such a lot of food and drink—and now my own children have to go hungry, miserable woman that I am!"

But Papa could not bear to see his wife in such distress. "No, no, Louise, don't blame yourself," he murmured gently. "If it weren't for the dry weather we would be all right. But if God will not send us rain, he will look after us some other way, for sure."

Bernadette believed this. Why should God not look after them? Did they not say the rosary together each night? Did not her mother share with the poor and also take a precious penny to light a candle in the church each Sunday? She herself spent many of her sleepless hours thinking of Jesus and praying to him to put a generous spirit into their landlord, so that he would not force them out of their home. She even told Jesus that she would not ask him to make her asthma better if her sacrifice could help soften the heart of Papa's cousin, Armand Soubirous.

In spite of the family's hopes and prayers, their milling business dwindled to nothing. The gabled windows of the house stared blankly at a silent yard. No clucking hens pecked for grain; no pigs squealed in the sty; no horse neighed in the barn. Worst of all, there was no merry jingling of harness bells, shouts of men or laughter of boisterous children coming to the mill.

Armand rode again into the mill yard on his white horse. Bernadette heard her father pleading with him. Her father, so proud and independent, was begging from his young cousin. "Please, Armand, give us more time. Think of the children. Where shall we go?"

Bernadette turned her face away. She could feel her father's humiliation.

Cousin Armand shrugged. He was going to get married, he said, and must have the mill for himself and his new wife.

The desperate family clung to their home for several more months. The weather improved but their business did not. Few of their old customers returned to have their grain ground to flour at the Boly Mill. The Soubirous owed far more rent than they could pay. They had to move out.

Bernadette, Toinette and Johnny helped their parents carry out their last few belongings and load them onto the old wooden cart. Then Bernadette slipped back into the empty house alone to say goodbye to the home where she had lived all her life. She looked for the last time around the large kitchen. The floor was swept, the room was bare. In her memory, she saw the colorful rag rugs her mother had hooked and the shining pine table where they had gathered for supper. She heard the crowing of the cuckoo clock counting the hours and could almost smell the wild flowers that had filled the glass vases.

Closing her eyes, she heard the murmur of the night prayers that rose each evening when the family knelt in front of the large crucifix over the fireplace. She saw the flicker of candlelight on the picture of the Madonna and the Child Jesus. At least these holy objects would go with them. There were some things so sacred that they could never be sold.

At last, she ran outdoors to join the others. The younger ones clung to her, tearful and scared. "I must be brave," she thought. She made up her mind that she would help her parents all she could, even if it meant that she could not go to school for awhile. Then she told the children a long, long story, about the wicked lord who had once lived in the Lourdes castle, and how he had surrendered his land to the Virgin Mary, Queen of Heaven. The story soothed Johnny and he stopped crying.

Meanwhile, Mama and Papa hauled the cart by hand to the home of Mama's mother, Claire Castérot. They would move into Grandmother's house to stay with her and Mama's unmarried older brother, John, and younger sisters, Basile and Lucile.

Months earlier, when Grandmother realized the Soubirous would lose the Boly Mill, she sold her home on the Forest Road and bought a small mill nearby, the Laborde Mill. She invited her daughter and son-in-law to help run this mill, although it was too small to support them all. Everyone would have to do odd jobs and work hard to make ends meet. Even so, as long as Grandmother had her health and strength, she would never let her daughter's family go without a decent place to live.

When the cart stopped, the children peered dolefully at their new home. Their parents felt nervous about moving into Grandmother's house. Would the rest of the family be willing to share with them? Would they be angry about squeezing in to make room?

Their heavy hearts were relieved when Grandmother rushed to greet them with open arms. Uncle John and the young aunts, Basile and Lucile, gathered around, shouting out their hellos. Uncle John helped Papa unload the cart, while the delicious aroma of Grandmother's cooking wafted from the stove.

Soon all were crowded around the kitchen table, tearing hungrily at the crisp little loaves of white bread, and eating bowls of Grandmother's delicious *cassoulet*, a mixture of beans with lamb and pork, baked in her own special sweet-smelling sauce. Nothing had ever tasted so good.

That night Bernadette felt contented and safe. Drifting off to sleep beside Toinette, she looked forward to the coming year. "I will go to school with Lucile and Toinette," she thought drowsily. "Papa will be happy working the mill with Uncle John, and Mama will not have to worry so much."

CHAPTER THREE

THE HAPPIEST CHRISTMAS

Christmas was coming, and the entire family busily prepared for the great day. Johnny helped Grandmother cut cookies into stars and hearts. Aunt Basile knitted secret gifts. Papa whittled pieces of wood in the evenings, and chuckled quietly when his little son demanded to know what he was carving.

Bernadette, Toinette and Aunt Lucile spent many evenings painting the *santons* bought at the market. These clay figurines represented all the characters the family would place in the nativity scene on their kitchen table at Christmas. Mary and Joseph would be close to the manger of the Baby Jesus, then the shepherds with their lambs, and the three wise kings with their camels.

Clay figures of each family member would also be around the crib to honor the newborn savior—Mama in her striped blue and white kerchief, Papa in his beret, Grandmother with her grey and black hair, and the rest of the family, old and young. Even the farmer would be represented with his horse and cart, along with the shopkeepers and officials, the priests, the emperor, and the empress in her feathered hat. Angels and patron saints could not be left out. All must be decorated by the family's busy fingers.

During the day Bernadette was left with her grandmother and little brother in the mill house. Once again her hopes of going to school had been dashed. She was dejected at having to stay home while her mother went to work and her sister was at school.

"Your turn will come," Mama promised, putting her arms around her unhappy daughter. Bernadette was not comforted. "Perhaps books will never be for me," she thought sadly.

That December, 1854, Pope Pius IX celebrated a magnificent ritual in Rome that seemed to have nothing to do with Bernadette's family. Yet that ceremony was destined to become very meaningful for them and for the people of Lourdes.

At the great domed Basilica of St. Peter's in the Vatican, the Pope proclaimed the dogma of the Immaculate Conception of the Virgin Mary, the mother of Jesus. He taught that Mary was full of divine grace and free of the stain of Original Sin from the moment of her conception, as most Catholics had believed since Jesus Christ founded the Church.

This solemn celebration was mostly ignored by the people of Lourdes. They were busy preparing for Christmas, and saw no reason to pay attention to a complicated pronouncement from Rome.

On that wondrous Christmas Eve, Mama and Papa forgot their troubles for awhile. With their children and the rest of the family, they joined in the procession to the huge nativity scene that the townsmen had built outside the church. Shepherds in wool hats and scarves led the procession, piping merry tunes;

cellists and fiddlers joined in; and the people sang carols about the well-loved story of Christ's birth. Their greetings to one another filled the frosty air.

Most of the townspeople assembled in the church for Midnight Mass. Father Peyramale and the other priests looked majestic in red and gold vestments. Hundreds of candles flickered in front of the altar and along the walls. Incense made the air hazy and fragrant. The choir burst into a mighty chorus singing *Gloria in Excelsis Deo,* Glory to God in the Highest, the song that the angels sang to the shepherds on the first Christmas night. The splendor of the ceremony awed Bernadette. She listened raptly when Father Peyramale read out the Gospel story of angels and shepherds gathering around the newborn savior.

All the children, and some of the grown-ups, were rather afraid of Father Peyramale. He was a huge man, with beetling eyebrows, a brusque manner and a voice like thunder. A story was told that he had once beaten off three wolves from his garden with his huge walking stick. Children thought he might use it on them if they annoyed him. In truth, he would not, for beneath his gruff manner he had a tender, fatherly heart.

Father Peyramale's booming voice softened as he read the story of the poor baby Jesus, born in the stable. Bernadette felt that her Redeemer entered more fully than usual into her spirit that night. She was happy and brimming with love.

After Mass, the children rushed home to see their gifts—rag dolls, new stockings and shawls for Bernadette and Toinette; a fine pair of little wooden horses with a cart for Johnny. In the long winter hours by the fire, Bernadette's busy hands had knit scarves for her mama and papa, mittens for her sister and brother. But the greatest surprise was what Mama had been knitting—a little sweater and bonnet. Yes. Soon there would be a new baby in the Soubirous household!

The whole family stayed up until dawn, singing and dancing. They relished the meat pies served with Grandma's special preserves, the toffee made by Aunts Basile and Lucile, the red apples bought especially for Christmas and the ginger cookies that Johnny had helped decorate. Each child drank a glass of water flavored with wine, the "pink water" that was such a special treat.

All her life Bernadette remembered this Christmas as the time when her family was happiest together.

Chapter Four

Grandmother's Life-Giving Love

In February, not long after Bernadette's eleventh birthday, a new little brother, Justin, was born. Mama could no longer go out to work, but spent hours by the fire nursing the fragile baby. Bernadette was fascinated by his tiny pink hands and feet. She loved to hold the infant and gaze into his shining face.

Then one day, Bernadette came down with a burning fever and painful stomach cramps. She was too sick to get out of bed. The family immediately knew the cause. Many children in the region had already died of cholera, a contagious and deadly disease.

At once Toinette ran to fetch the doctor. Aunt Lucile hurried to ask the priest to say a Mass for Bernadette. The family lit the blessed candles at the home altar and took turns in keeping up a constant stream of prayer. Bernadette was only vaguely aware of what was happening around her. She drifted in and out of a delirium that was like a strange dream.

Once she saw the kind, bearded face of Doctor Dozous leaning over her. Then she dimly heard him speaking to her grandmother, who hovered nearby. "No one must come near her except you," he warned

Grandmother. "You must wash and disinfect anything that touches Bernadette. Otherwise the other children will get sick too."

For weeks, Bernadette knew little except her grandmother's soothing hands, her crooning voice, and the blessed relief of cool water washing her burning body and aching head. She could hardly even swallow the herbal tea Grandmother prepared to ease her stomach cramps.

Bernadette was so tired and full of pain she could not lift her head from the pillow. As she drifted in and out of consciousness, the sick girl occasionally heard the murmur of prayer, the clatter of dishes, and the thin cry of the new baby. At times she glimpsed a heavenly world, full of light and beauty. She longed to enter that blissful kingdom, but she felt her family's love pulling her back, and knew that she must remain in this world.

Only afterward did Bernadette learn how much her grandmother had done. The older woman had neglected everything else to care for her, keeping watch day and night, bathing her and coaxing her back to life with her healing hands and the caressing murmur of her voice.

Bernadette awoke to hear the March wind rattling the windows. She was exhausted, but she came out of her delirium and recognized her surroundings. The first thing she felt was a deep gratitude for the woman who had nursed her during all her pain and confusion. Grandmother clasped Bernadette's small weak body in her strong arms, weeping and thanking God for sparing the girl's life.

Bernadette's wonderful recovery filled the whole family with joy. Even so, Mama and Papa had to go out to work as usual, and Grandmother was left to nurse her back to full health.

That spring and summer Bernadette felt weak and weary. Her stomach often ached. Her greatest pleasure was to sit in the shade of the chestnut trees caring for baby Justin. During her long months of convalescence, Bernadette learned many things from Grandmother, who taught her legends and songs, traditional recipes for tasty foods, and how to find and prepare medicines from the herbs that grew in the region. In caring for her two brothers while their parents worked, Bernadette found that she had the art of storytelling and the healing hands of the women in her family.

Early in October, the wheel of time brought autumn around once more. Like the leaves lying dry and brown on the ground, Grandmother was near the end of her life. She panted for breath when she carried heavy pails of water from the well. Her wrinkled face was grey and tired, but she continued to work late into the night, washing the floor and setting the bread dough to rise.

Early one morning Grandmother called for Bernadette's mother. "Louise!" she cried out in a voice that alarmed the whole household. They all rushed to her bedside. She sat up and smiled at them. She joined in their prayers, but gazed over their heads and stretched out her hands. Then she lay back and fell peacefully into her final sleep.

The family remained for many hours by her bedside, mourning the loss of their beloved Mother and Grandmother. Bernadette, especially, felt bereft. One of the main supports of her life was gone.

Grandmother left some money to each of her children. God knows how she had pinched pennies to save enough to make life easier for them after her death. Because of her careful planning, Papa and Mama now had enough money to start a new life.

Papa quickly found a small mill to rent in the village of Arcizac, three miles away from Lourdes on the Forest Road. The mill was a separate building from the house, so the noise and vibrations of the grinding millstones did not disturb the household. The family's new home was located on the banks of the crystal clear Magnas River and was surrounded by trees golden in the autumn sun.

Bernadette was charmed by their tiny cottage in the woods. She picked delicate wild flowers and reverently arranged them on the home altar. There the family gathered each evening by candlelight to pray the rosary.

At first Papa set off to the mill in the morning whistling merrily, and came home in the evening full of plans to enlarge the house and to make it more comfortable. As time went by, his smile faded and his brow became furrowed with worry. The mill did not have many customers. Larger mills closer to Lourdes got most of the trade. Mama had learned to be careful with money, but still they could not afford to buy enough food. Both she and Papa once more had to find odd jobs on the neighboring farms or in the town of Lourdes.

While Mama worked on farms picking fruit and vegetables, Bernadette looked after the house, her younger sister and her two small brothers, Johnny and Justin. Although Mama was paid only a few cents a day for her work, she often brought home baskets of fruit and eggs, vegetables and discarded cuts of meat. These filled the soup pot. Mama promised that when the harvest season was over, she would stay home with the two little boys, and Bernadette could go to school with Toinette.

It was not to be. November ushered in a cruel winter. Biting winds pressed against the flimsy cottage, rattling the windows and sending in cold drafts. The large stacks of wood they gathered and piled in the stove were not enough to warm the house. The poor Soubirous family often ate their supper huddled around the fire and wrapped in blankets. Toinette went to school each morning, bundled up in a woolen hat, scarf, and a hooded cape. Bernadette remained home, plagued by her old enemies, asthma and bronchitis. Fits of coughing racked her body. Her bout with cholera had weakened her and made these attacks worse than ever.

The young girl's hopes of being a schoolgirl blew away with the wintry winds.

CHAPTER FIVE

AUNT BERNARDE'S HOUSE

One day, in this scene of melancholy, Aunt Bernarde appeared like a fairy godmother. She brought bundles of firewood, clothes, blankets and a large basket that contained a chicken, sausages, cheese, vegetables and luscious-looking cakes.

The Soubirous house was soon ringing with shouts and laughter, heated by a crackling fire, and filled with the good aromas of chicken stewing and biscuits baking in the oven. Even Mama was lively and happy, bustling around the kitchen with her sister, and joking and laughing as in the old days. When Papa came home from his delivery job, he was cheered by the unexpected warmth and good food.

Bernadette ate very little of the dinner. Between spasms of coughing, she leaned her head wearily on her hand. Aunt Bernarde looked at her goddaughter in alarm.

"Why how pale and tired you look, child," she exclaimed. "You must try to eat more so you will grow strong."

Aunt Bernarde was a tall, good-looking woman with all the self-confidence that Mama lacked. Her first husband, a farmer, died shortly after their marriage. She soon married again, this time to a wine-merchant, Jean-Marie Nicolau, who traveled a good deal. She knew how to manage alone and considered herself able to cope with any situation. As the eldest daughter in the family, she felt it her right and duty to look after her sisters and their families after their mother's death.

"Bernadette's digestion has never been good since she had the cholera," Mama explained. "And her chest is weaker. She gets terrible attacks of asthma and bronchitis, so she needs lots of rest. But I'm sure she will get well again when the weather warms up."

Aunt Bernarde was not convinced. "Bernadette must come home with me, Louise," she declared. "She will be able to take it easy at our house, with nothing to do except play with the children when she feels up to it. Plenty of good food and warmth will do wonders for her."

"That is good of you, Bernarde," said Mama gratefully. Then she turned to her daughter and questioned, "You would like to go with your godmother, would you not, Bernadette?"

Bernadette looked earnestly at the two women. "Will I be able to go to school?" she asked.

Aunt Bernarde laughed. "Of course you will, little goose," she said lightly. "But first you must get well."

When supper was finished and the dishes done, Papa gently wrapped Bernadette in a blanket and carried her to the coach that Aunt Bernarde had arranged to be waiting at the door. The young girl's heart ached as she waved good-bye, but she was sure God would make her well at her aunt's house so that at last she could study the catechism and make her First Communion.

Bernadette soon settled into the prosperous life at the Nicolaus' home with her Uncle Jean-Marie, her Aunt Bernarde and their two little children. The household also included Bernadette's young unmarried aunts, Basile and Lucile, who treated Bernadette like a sister. They shared their clothes with her and related the latest news from town.

Bernadette began to feel like her old self; her keen sense of humor and gift of mimicry returned. To the delight of all, she would amusingly imitate the gestures and speech of the baker, the soldiers, the owner of the dress shop and other people they knew. This ability also made her an excellent nanny. Aunt Bernarde's children loved to play dress-up with her and to hear her stories and songs.

During the day, Aunt Basile was at work, Aunt Lucile at school, and Aunt Bernarde was usually busy in the wine shop. Bernadette's godmother neglected to send her niece to school regularly. Instead, she expected the girl to be a babysitter for her own small children. On the days Bernadette was allowed to go to school, she sat in the lower ranks with the younger children because she had not yet learned to read.

Her friend, Catherine, was disturbed about this. "It's a shame, Bernadette. You are just as clever as anyone, but Sister thinks you are stupid because you can't read and haven't learned to speak proper French. If I were you, I would just tell that old Auntie of yours that she must let you come to school every day."

Bernadette wanted to argue with her Aunt Bernarde about it, but she knew she owed her health, and perhaps even her life, to her godmother's care. So she made up her mind not to complain and to show her thanks by making her little cousins happy. Although she always had a quick retort when she was teased by the other girls, she tried hard not to answer back when her aunt scolded her.

Evenings with the family were full of gossip and droll comments. Uncle Nicolau was generous and enjoyed bringing home little gifts from his travels. One day he brought some rings for "his girls." Bernadette's ring was too small, but she was so pleased to have some jewelry that she squeezed it onto her little finger. Her finger swelled up and turned blue. She tugged and tugged, but in vain. The ring was stuck. She began crying with pain.

"I am sorry, Bernadette," Uncle Nicolau said contritely. "I did not realize you were getting to be such a big girl." He quickly and carefully filed the ring off of Bernadette's finger. "I will get you a larger one next time," he promised.

"No thank you, Uncle," she said firmly, looking at her swollen finger. "I never want to wear a ring again." Just the same, she felt disappointed. She liked pretty things.

When spring came, Bernadette longed to return to her own family's little home in the woods. In her imagination, she played with Johnny and Toinette in the forest or sat by the stream with baby Justin. "I must go home now, Aunt Bernarde," she announced one morning.

Her aunt was infuriated. "What!" she exclaimed. "After all I have done for you. Now you want to leave the care of my little children to strangers."

"But Auntie," said Bernadette. "Johnny and Justin also need someone to care for them. Mama must go to work or they won't have enough to eat. Please, don't be angry," she pleaded. "I have to go."

"Ridiculous," her aunt retorted. "Toinette is nine years old. She is perfectly able to stay home and help. How ungrateful you are, Bernadette. Well, if you insist on leaving, don't beg me to take you back when you get sick again."

Bernadette was sorry to upset her aunt, but she insisted on having her own way since she was sure she was doing the right thing. Her Uncle Nicolau agreed to drive her home. Next day she kissed her cousins good-bye and climbed into the cart beside him for the bumpy journey over the Forest Road to the village of Arcizac.

The air smelled of fruit blossoms and fresh grass. Puffy clouds drifted lazily across the blue sky. Bees hummed, tall poplar trees rustled and the fresh spring breeze swept her hair. "I'm going home!" Bernadette said to herself. "Home, home, home," the wagon wheels seemed to repeat.

Soon, her mama was hugging and exclaiming over her. "Let me look at you, Bernadette," she said, running her hands over her daughter's shining brown hair. "Ah, the roses are back in your cheeks. How healthy you look now. It did you good to go."

Her tall quiet Papa, so different from the rotund Uncle Nicolau, lifted her up and swung her around, both of them laughing. Toinette gleefully pulled at Bernadette to come outside and play. Even Justin toddled over and reached up his little arms to her. Johnny, playing with his stick men, pretended to ignore her. He was still angry with her for going away. But, at the same time, he couldn't wait to show her his new slingshot and how well he could use it.

The whole family celebrated by having a picnic outdoors on the banks of the river. Although the water was cold from the melting snow upstream, the bright sun warmed the air. They spread a rug on the ground, and enjoyed this special time of togetherness as they ate from the basket of food and drank the pale wine that Bernadette had coaxed her uncle to bring with them.

The next morning Mama left the house to work on a nearby farm and Papa went out to find odd jobs in the town. When Toinette set off for school, Bernadette tidied up the house and spent the afternoon playing with her little brothers by the stream and in the woods. To keep Johnny from wandering away, she told him children's tales, like *Little Red Riding Hood*. This made his brown eyes glow.

"I would not let the big wolf get me," he said fiercely. "I would run and fetch Papa if one dared to come near us. Papa would hit him with a big stick." Just the same, he stayed close by Bernadette.

On sunny afternoons, Bernadette took her brothers for walks in the village of Arcizac. She made friends with the villagers, especially another girl, Victorine, who also took care of a younger brother. Victorine sometimes gave candies to the little boys, if they were good.

Those spring and summer days spent amid the beauty and mystery of the woods helped Bernadette become stronger and more self-reliant. She was not lonely, but was always glad to see her friends from Lourdes when they came to visit. On Sundays the family walked to Mass and then spent the afternoon in the forest or fishing in the stream. These were the happiest days Bernadette had known since her grandmother died.

Her joy ended all too soon. There was no second summer for the Soubirous family in their little mill house in Arcizac. The mill did not get enough business to pay the rent, and, by autumn, the family was penniless once more. They had to leave the Arcizac Mill and their little cottage. They prayed to God to help them find a shelter from the cold winter winds. Where they could find such a place they did not know, for they now had no money left.

CHAPTER SIX

LIVING IN A DUNGEON

In late October, the Soubirous family searched frantically for a place they could call home. The chill wind of poverty swept them from one hovel to another. Like shriveled leaves that fall from the trees and are blown aimlessly until they land in the gutter, the family finally settled in a dungeon.

This dank underground room was formerly a jail, a place so nasty that even criminals were no longer kept there. It was at the end of a stonemason's workshop and under the apartment of François' cousin, André Sejoux.

Into this deserted dungeon, the humiliated household unloaded their few belongings and set up a home. The room measured only twelve by fifteen feet. Its window faced a smelly courtyard and let in no sun. The flagstone floor was rough and cracked. In spite of the family's efforts to clean up, green fungus clung to the damp stone walls.

The dungeon had a few advantages. It gave them shelter, and the owner, André Sejoux, did not charge any rent. It was also very, very private. Neighbors and friends, knowing the family's poverty, did not often drop in for a visit.

In spite of all their troubles, the Soubirous family did not lose their Catholic faith. They hung the large crucifix, a cherished heirloom and the only object of beauty or value now left from their former life, over the fireplace where they gathered each evening in prayer. Although they lived hand-to-mouth, they trusted their heavenly Father for their daily bread.

Sometimes Toinette and Bernadette squabbled with each other, but they never heard their parents quarrel. Mama knew how to make peace among the children and to win their loving respect. Although theirs was the poorest home in the town of Lourdes, they were rich in love. Poverty and suffering had not broken the family's spirit. This impressed their landlord and upstairs relative, André Sejoux, who occasionally invited them to have supper with his family.

Each morning Papa went out to search for any paying work he could find. By turns, he was a deliveryman for the baker and stagecoach driver for the postmaster, but there was no steady job for him. Sometimes he drove fashionable ladies to popular health spas in the region. Since Papa was always considerate and courteous, he occasionally received generous tips from these ladies. On many days, however, he walked from one shop to another, pleading in vain for any work that would bring in a few pennies.

François sorely missed the fellowship of other men. Bernadette knew that it wrenched his heart to pass the tavern where his old friends sat drinking and exchanging news and jokes in loud voices. He longed to join them, but seldom splurged on a glass of wine.

For in spite of all his effort, Papa earned very little money. When he could not find work, he spent the day in bed, refusing to eat lest his children go hungry. Bernadette tried to entice him to share her white bread and the watered wine that the doctor ordered for her delicate stomach. But Papa just groaned and turned his face to the wall.

Mama also had to work at odd jobs. She became, in turn, a cleaning woman, a washerwoman and a farm worker. Although she received little pay, her employers often gave her leftover food to bring home. Sometimes they gave her a box of used clothing, or allowed her to use their soap for washing her own children's clothes.

Each day Toinette ran up the steps of their dreary home and set off for her heated schoolroom. Bernadette had to remain behind to look after her brothers. She had given up hope of going to school. At thirteen, she began to fear that she was too old to learn.

Bernadette loved both of her brothers. The frail Justin adored her and she found it easy to look after him, but she worried about Johnny. The hungry boy frequently roamed around town in search of something to eat.

One day the kindly Mrs. Lestrade discovered Johnny eating candle wax from the floor of the church, so she invited him to her house for a mid-day meal. He accepted her offer, but ate outside on her porch, and refused to enter the house or tell her his name. His papa had warned him that he must never beg. When Bernadette found out about this charity, she was ashamed that her brother had to be fed by strangers; but she also felt sorry for her "little guy," as she called him, who was always so famished.

Some days Justin toddled along with Bernadette to see the town sights. She showed him the courthouse, the market, the castle where the soldiers in their colorful uniforms paraded up and down. Often they went inside the church. Here all was silence and beauty. Bernadette would pray and show her little brother the many statues and the images in the stained glass windows.

They could not linger in church very long because these walks had a practical purpose: Bernadette was looking for items left lying around on the street that she could sell. Justin's tiny hands helped pick up rags and bones for her basket.

At the end of their hunting expedition, they carried this pitiful collection to the dark, cluttered second-hand shop. A little bell tinkled as they opened the door, and an old woman, Alexine Baron, peered at them over her counter. She fussed over their findings as if unable to make up her mind, but finally threw them into her bag and gave Bernadette a couple of pennies from her cash box. Then Bernadette and Justin hurried to the baker's shop to buy stale bread and rolls with the money.

On one of these outings Bernadette and Justin passed Mrs. Jacomet, the police inspector's wife, walking with her five-year-old daughter, Amanda. The little girl was carrying a small pair of stockings, her first knitting achievement. Amanda had told her mother that she would give the stockings to the first poor child she met on the street. When the girl saw Bernadette and her little brother, she ran up and presented them with the stockings. Bernadette received the gift gratefully. No longer would Justin's frail legs turn blue in the winter wind.

For Bernadette, the worst part of their poverty was not the hunger and cold, or the humiliation of being a scavenger. The most detestable part was the ugliness of the dungeon. Lying in bed at night, she would look at the patches of green mold on the walls. These became terrifying in the flickering candle light. The blotches seemed to come alive, changing to brilliant magenta and lurid orange, and threatening her with fierce gestures. Then she would cling in fright to her sister sleeping peacefully beside her in the same bed. Toinette would murmur soothingly to her. Although she was not very sensitive, Toinette was fond of Bernadette, who had always shared everything with her. She felt pity for her sister's sufferings.

At other times, Bernadette would wake with a coughing fit from her asthma and bronchitis. Then Mama would rise wearily from her short sleep and brew a cup of tisane, a healing herbal tea. She would sit by the fire holding her daughter wrapped in a blanket. The warm tea, the hum of the kettle, the gentle hands and lilting voice of her mama would lull Bernadette back to sleep.

The grey cold of winter finally gave way to spring. Yellow-green leaves sprouted on trees. The streams gurgled with water from the melting snow in the mountains. On Sundays, their day of rest, the Soubirous family got away from the dungeon for a few hours. After Mass, if the weather was fine, they walked around the hills and meadows and into the woods where they could hunt and fish. When the weather improved, extra jobs became available to François and Louise, so they were able to earn a bit more money.

Just as the cold grip of poverty loosened, tragedy struck. Papa was put in jail! One afternoon a policeman appeared at the door along with the baker, Mr. Maisongrosse. This baker was a fat man, who should have been as jolly as Santa Claus, but was just the opposite. He claimed that two of his bags of flour were missing. Since Papa had been his deliveryman at times, the baker accused him of stealing them. A suspicious, stupid and stingy man, Mr. Maisongrosse did not believe that anyone could be trusted.

Papa, the most honest of men, was outraged. He loudly declared his innocence. He was insulted; his honor was more important than his life.

"Look around you," he roared. "Do you see any bags of flour? I invite you to search every corner of this room and tell me if you can find even a cup of flour. Go ahead, search."

Of course, the policeman could find no such thing. He was baffled and shamefaced. To save his pride, he looked for some excuse to arrest François. Finally, he spotted an old board in the yard that the poor man had brought home after finding it leaning up against a public building. The previous owner had abandoned it there for anyone to pick up. The policeman charged him with stealing this piece of lumber and prepared to lead him off to jail.

Mama and the children were weeping and shouting. They felt disgraced and terrified. Nevertheless, Papa spoke with great dignity to his children.

"My children," he said, "you must never believe that your father is a thief. Never, ever would I steal, even though we might all starve." He squatted down in front of little Johnny. "You must be a man, my son. Look after Mama while I am gone."

Then, François stood up and tried to comfort his distraught family. "I will soon be back, never fear. They will not be able to prove that I stole this board. It is true I am a miller without a mill. But I am not a thief and I am not a beggar. Always remember that. May God protect you all while I am gone."

Johnny threw his arms around Papa, sobbing. The other children also clung to him, crying as if their hearts would break. The policeman looked away in embarrassment.

At that moment, Mama erupted in a rage at the policeman. "Fool! Idiot! Oh, you wicked, wicked man!" she berated. "You want to take a father away from his children for nothing at all. Ask the good Lord to forgive you." Then she turned her ire on the baker. "And you, gross baker man. Stealing, you say? It is you who are stealing, stealing a father away from his family."

Her shrieks rose louder and louder. She grabbed her stick and began lashing at the policeman, hitting him on his head and shoulders. The affronted officer promptly seized François by the arm and, in sight of the curious neighbors, marched him like a criminal through the streets of Lourdes, to the jail.

Mama sat on her stool, dazed with anguish. "He will lose his mind," she kept repeating. "He will lose his mind."

Bernadette did not know which of her parents she pitied more, and her own grief was almost unbearable. From her heart arose the age-old lament of the suffering, "Dear God, why have you let this happen to us?" as she gazed at the dark walls of the dungeon, at the scanty lunch laid out on the table, at the sobbing children and her dear mama, stunned by this disaster.

Anger against the baker spurred Bernadette to action. "No one is going to bring our family to beggary by putting Papa in jail for no reason," she thought.

Whispering comforting words to the children, she made them sit down and served them hot soup. She prepared a cup of soothing tea for her mother. Then, picking up her basket, she marched to the baker's shop and ordered two loaves of bread.

"We will pay you when Papa comes home," she said sternly. "They will soon let him out, you know, because he has done nothing wrong—even though some people find it in their hearts to call him a thief."

Ashamed, the baker admitted he had found the flour and asked her pardon. "I forgive you, since Our Lord tells us to forgive our enemies," said Bernadette. "But you must pray for God's pardon, Mr. Maisongrosse, for God is not pleased with you today."

In spite of this bold show of confidence, Bernadette feared that the family might indeed starve with Papa in jail. Luckily, their neighbors were sympathetic, for they all knew that François was no thief. Though they were poor, many brought over food that they pretended they had left over.

Aunt Bernarde, who had been very angry with Bernadette for returning home the previous summer, forgot her grievance and brought over eggs and firewood, lamb stew with dumplings and even a bottle of wine. Mama put the wine away for the day when Papa got out of jail.

Nine days later, Papa was set free and came home. No charges were laid against him. The neighbors ran to the dungeon to congratulate him. They brought enough eggs, cheese, wine, bread and sweet cakes to have a party. Papa was pleased by their faith in him and heartily joined in the fun, although he knew some would always gossip about him. He had changed, but he had not lost his mind, as Mama had feared.

Once more, he gathered his family around him, kissing and hugging each one. He told them how he had missed them. "But God was with me," he assured them. "And from now on, I am not going to worry or complain. I know I'm not providing enough for you, but I will do my best. We must all trust in God. I am certain that He will bring us out of this poor cellar, if only we leave it to Him."

When Bernadette heard her papa say this, she felt a deeper respect for him. She saw quiet hope in his eyes, and she knew that his time in jail had strengthened his faith.

Bernadette always had a profound love of Jesus, though she seldom talked about it. For his sake she never wanted to do anything bad, although she sometimes lost her temper with Toinette and was quick to answer back when other children hurt her feelings.

This time of hardship helped prepare Bernadette to be the person God needed for the great work ahead of her. She was learning patience and trust. She was learning to sacrifice her own desires for others, and to endure pain and hunger without complaint. God would indeed answer her father's prayer, but in an unexpected way, and only when Bernadette was ready. Her life was about to change once more.

CHAPTER SEVEN

OUT ON THE FARM

Toinette and Bernadette woke up early and excitedly on the Feast of Corpus Christi in June 1857, for this was the day of Toinette's First Holy Communion. The nuns at the convent had loaned her a white dress and veil and a white cape. She was also to wear a blue sash because she belonged to the Sodality of the Children of Mary, a group of young girls dedicated to the Blessed Virgin. She would walk with that group in the procession after Mass. The priest, Father Peyramale, would carry the Blessed Sacrament in its large round monstrance.

Bernadette helped Toinette get ready. She brushed her sister's dark brown curls and adjusted her veil carefully. While placing a wreath of white roses on the younger girl's head, she commented softly, "You look like an angel, Toinette."

Then Bernadette turned away from her sister, quelling a pang of envy and wondering when her own turn would come. She dressed the two little boys, who were still playing on the bed. Of course, the whole family must be well prepared for this sacred occasion.

The Corpus Christi Mass at St. Peter's, the parish church in Lourdes, was a special ritual. The choir and organ filled the arched ceiling of the church with glorious music. The ranks of altar boys wore red cassocks beneath their starched and lacy white surplices. Under the watchful eye of their director, Mr. Savignac, they managed to stand straight and fairly still through the whole long ceremony.

To help the Soubirous family celebrate, their old friends, the Lagües, came into Lourdes from Bartrès. After the religious festivities, the two families shared the picnic lunch the Lagües brought from the farm.

For two years, Bernadette had not seen her foster mother, Marie, who was busy looking after her own large family. The stout, hearty farmwoman was horrified by the poverty of her old friends. She was especially distressed to see the change in Bernadette, her foster child.

"Louise," she exclaimed, "our little girl is thin and pale. Let her come to live with us on the farm. She will soon get strong and well with good food and fresh country air. Besides," she promised, "we will send her to school regularly. In her spare time, she can earn her keep by helping me with the children."

Mama hesitated. What would she do without her oldest daughter? She was thirteen years old and a big help to the family. Still, she reflected, Toinette was ten years old and could do her share now. Toinette and Johnny were at school all day, and a neighbor would look after little Justin when needed. Mama looked to Papa for his decision. He nodded his acceptance. Her parents could see that Bernadette was wasting away in the dungeon without enough proper food.

A few weeks later Jeanne Marie Garros, the Lagües' maid, drove a horse and cart into Lourdes to pick up Bernadette and bring her and her few belongings up the road to Bartrès. Bernadette was reluctant to leave her own family once again, but she was eager to go to school. Besides, she liked the Lagües and had many fond memories of visiting their family.

The open countryside and the farm were a welcome change compared to life in the dreary dungeon. Everyone worked hard, but they also had fun. Bernadette enjoyed playing hide-and-seek with the farm children, romping with the sheep dog, Pigou, and swinging on a rope hanging from a huge tree.

Bernadette and Josèphe "Josephine" Lagües, her foster sister, wandered in the meadows, gathering wild daisies that they wove into chains while chatting under the shady trees. Bernadette was reminded of her own sister, Toinette, when she looked at Josephine's brown face, curly black hair and bubbly ways.

On Sundays, the whole family went to Mass in the parish church of St. John the Baptist in Bartrès. Although the church was small, it contained life-size marble statues of the Baptism of Jesus, an ornate altar and richly colored windows. After Mass, with other children of the village, Bernadette studied the catechism in the priest's stone house near the church.

The heavy summer work of the farm was mixed with laughter and good-natured teasing. Bernadette, out in the sun and wind much of the time, lost her pallor. Her olive skin became tinged with rose and her face became round and pretty. The warm-hearted maid, Jeanne Marie Garros, gladly shared her bedroom with Bernadette. Even though she missed her own family, Bernadette became used to her life with the Lagües.

After the lambs were weaned, her foster father, Basil Lagües, told Bernadette to take charge of caring for them. Each day, with the help of the sheep dog, Pigou, she herded the bleating animals to the nearby Puyono pasture, and watched over them until evening. Instead of joining the family for the big dinner at noon, she brought bread and cheese to eat in the meadow.

At first, Bernadette enjoyed watching the lambs frisk and butt their heads against each other. She chose the smallest lamb to be her own pet and fed the tiny creature with violet leaves and tender grasses. But with only the dog and the lambs for company, she eventually grew lonesome.

"Oh, well," she thought, "it won't be long. When school begins I shall have lots of friends to play with."

Finally, the long-anticipated day arrived. The village school opened in September—but Papa Lagües refused to let her go. "I need you to look after the lambs," he stated curtly, ignoring her distress. "Mama Lagües can teach you the catechism in the evening when the work is done."

Stunned at this betrayal, Bernadette fled to her room.

Chapter Eight

Unpaid Servant

That September, Mama Lagües' treatment of Bernadette changed completely. No longer like a mother with a beloved daughter, she became cold and demanding. The attitude of the rest of the family also transformed from affectionate to contemptuous. Jeanne-Marie, the hard-working maid, was the only one who remained sympathetic.

Bernadette had to rise very early each morning to dress and feed the children. After her day in the pasture, she helped with the evening work and put the little ones to bed.

She went out with the lambs and the dog, Pigou, every day. During rainy weather, they found shelter in the stone shepherd's hut. It was dark inside and Bernadette could hear the mice scurrying inside its low, thatched roof.

When a violent storm threatened one day, Basil ordered Bernadette to bring the lambs back to the farm. To return, they had to cross a creek. This was usually a mere trickle of water, but heavy rain had turned it into a fast-moving torrent. The lambs were afraid to cross. They bleated piteously on the water's edge, their white coats torn by the wind.

Bernadette closed her eyes, almost in a panic. She said an earnest prayer, then picked up her pet lamb and bravely stepped into the water. Her long, worn skirt clung wetly to her legs. Her shawl flapped in the windstorm. Pigou ran around the lambs to keep them together, barking furiously.

Suddenly the stream stopped flowing, leaving a path through the riverbed for the flock to cross, driven on by Pigou. This astounded the neighbors, who were watching from their windows. When all were safely on the other side, the creek overflowed its banks again. The people in the village informed the Lagües about this apparent miracle, but when the family questioned Bernadette, she just smiled.

"Almost everyone loved her," Jeanne-Marie, the kindly maid, reported in later years. If so, they had a strange way of showing it. Bernadette worked all day, every day except Sundays, but she was given no money, and had to wear the same worn clothes she had brought with her. She was not allowed to take catechism lessons and went to school only when the weather was too stormy to take the lambs to pasture.

Mass on Sundays was her only outing. She loved the beauty of the church and the singing of the choir. Sometimes she watched the red and gold sanctuary lamp swaying back and forth on its long chain. She pondered how the light flickering in the lamp silently proclaimed the presence of Jesus in the tabernacle. How she longed to receive Him in Holy Communion.

The Lagües' indifference and coldness towards Bernadette surprised Marie Lagües' brother, Father Jean-Louis Aravant, a priest who came to visit the Lagües home. When he saw that Bernadette was being treated as a servant, not being sent to school and not even learning her catechism, he scolded his sister, Marie, and her husband, Basil. "You are responsible for her before God," he chided. "You should treat her as your own child. At the very least she must learn her religion."

Shame-faced, Marie agreed. But her husband would not hear of it. He insisted that Marie could teach Bernadette in the evenings. Yet by nightfall, the girl was too tired to learn. Marie was a poor teacher and could scarcely read herself. She criticized Bernadette for not being able to memorize the words of the catechism, even though they were written in a style of French that was very different from Bernadette's local dialect.

One evening Marie threw down the catechism book in frustration. "You are stupid, Bernadette. You will never learn!" she exclaimed. Bernadette, overcome with weariness, laid her head on her foster-mother's shoulder and put her arms around the woman's neck. "I'm sorry, I'm so sorry, Mama Lagües," she apologized. "I give you so much trouble."

Marie pushed her away. "Don't be foolish. Get to bed now. You won't be fit to work tomorrow if you don't get some sleep."

It was a long time before Bernadette could fall asleep that night. She felt bitterly let down. Even so, she made up her mind not to complain. Since God permitted all this to happen, there must be a reason.

In the grassy hills of the meadow, with its ever changing skies and towering trees, Bernadette found consolation. She imagined the clouds were heavenly lambs herded by the angels. She learned to appreciate the beauty of nature and thanked God, who had created all the loveliness around her. She gathered stones, and in the shade of a large tree, built a tiny altar with a picture of the Madonna and Child on it. Here she knelt and said her rosary in the hot afternoons when the lambs were sleeping.

At times, Bernadette was bored, but she had to stay alert to make sure the lambs did not wander away. She kept herself occupied by knitting and mending or searching for nuts in the fragrant grass.

When the weather turned cold, Bernadette spent more time in the shepherd's hut, sheltered from the wind. She knew that the lambs would soon be sold. What would happen to her then, she wondered. Would the Lagües ever send her to school? She doubted it. Sometimes she seemed to hear God's voice within, urging her to return home to Lourdes.

One day Bernadette's cousin, Jeanne Védère, drove her horse and cart all the way from Tarbes to spend the day with her. Jeanne was irate when she heard how the Lagües were mistreating her cousin.

Jeanne had always been Bernadette's favorite confidante, the only one with whom she shared the secrets of her heart. She told Jeanne her feeling that God wished her to go back to Lourdes and begged her to persuade her papa to come and take her home. Jeanne did as Bernadette requested. Bernadette's papa walked out to the farm to fetch his daughter, but when he saw that her face had become plump and rosy, he refused to take her back to the poverty of the dungeon.

"The Laguës will not send me to school," she implored. "I am nearly fourteen. I must learn my catechism so I can receive Holy Communion. Please take me back with you."

Papa shook his head. He feared that the harsh conditions of life in the dungeon would drag Bernadette's health down again. He could not bear to see his child suffering or listen to her gasping for breath in the damp cellar that was all he could offer for a home. He left her with the Laguës.

Even as chill winter winds swept through the valley, Bernadette continued to take the lambs to the meadow each day. Basil Laguës would not allow her to go home, not even for Christmas.

One Sunday in January, just after her fourteenth birthday, Bernadette took her future into her own hands. She informed Marie and Basil that she was going to visit her family. Seeing her determination, Basil reluctantly agreed. "But remember," he barked, "you must come back first thing tomorrow morning."

Bernadette did not answer. She had made up her mind that she would never come back, and nothing was going to change that. When she arrived in Lourdes, she told her parents that she had come home to stay.

"The Lagües will never let me go to catechism classes. I must learn so that I can make my First Communion this June," she declared firmly.

In spite of their fear for her health, Bernadette's parents accepted her back home and allowed her to attend school regularly. At first, she sat with the smallest children and her teacher was often impatient with her. This nun was a newcomer to Lourdes and did not know Bernadette. She was an imperious woman who liked to keep her pupils under strict control. She tried to be saintly but had little understanding of the problems of the poor.

"Bernadette," she asked one day, when her new student could not answer a catechism question, "Are you too lazy to study, or are you just stupid?"

"Oh, I am very stupid, Sister," Bernadette replied, honestly believing it must be true since her foster mother had said so. Her teacher considered this an impudent answer. The nun was about to punish her when her little sister, Toinette, stood up for her.

"Please, don't be cross with Bernadette, Sister. She has been sick and has had to help Mama at home. She has never had time to learn to read."

When the teacher realized that Bernadette had been deprived of schooling for so many years, she asked one of the sisters at the convent to give her private reading lessons. Under this excellent teaching, Bernadette quickly learned to read simple words. Now she could study on her own and make up for lost time.

Still, her teacher continued to dislike the poorly clothed, but pert and lively Bernadette. The young girl's life with her family in the dungeon was also far from easy. Yet these sufferings were preparing Bernadette for an extraordinary grace and a great mission.

CHAPTER NINE

AN UNFORGETTABLE MORNING

Mist lay over the town of Lourdes. It clung to the spire of the church where bells rang to call the faithful to Mass. It softened the light of morning candles shining from windows. Neighbors scarcely recognized one another on the streets as they trudged along in the chilly fog.

In the dungeon, the morning began like every other. Yet, February 11, 1858, is known by devout Catholics all over the world because of what happened to Bernadette that day.

Mama threw a few sticks on the fire, bringing a little warmth and light into the gloomy room. "I must go and pick up some wood in the forest," she told her children, while she washed her skinny arms and gaunt face. "You girls will have to look after your brothers."

Bernadette remembered when her mother's arms had been round and firm, her lips full and red, her blue eyes sparkling. A desire to protect her mama sprang into the girl's heart.

"I'll go," she offered, pulling on her skirt and slipping into the blouse her mother had washed and ironed the previous day. She and Toinette had been snuggling in bed to keep warm. Her sister now sat up in bed, shivering.

"I'll go too," said Toinette, brushing the curls out of her eyes and sliding off the bed.

Mama willingly accepted their generous offer. Papa was home and could mind the little boys for a while. "You must wear stockings, Bernadette, and the warm cape," she said. "You were coughing last night and it is cold out."

"Oh Mama," Bernadette protested, "I went out in all weather without any stockings when I was at the Lagües farm." But she obeyed, and put on her stockings.

Quickly the two girls ate a stale roll and drank a cup of hot herbal tea. They were on their way out the door when Jeanne "Baloum" Labadie, a friend of Toinette's, burst in. She was a rough and energetic girl.

When Toinette told her friend that she and Bernadette were going out to gather firewood, Baloum commented, "Well, I might as well go with you."

Mama gave Baloum a disapproving look, tied a kerchief over her head, and set off to her job of cleaning house.

Bernadette put on the white hooded cape and all three girls set out in the fog toward the Forest Road. Their wooden shoes slipped on the wet cobblestone streets that sloped down to the Gave River.

At the Old Bridge, they passed a pitiable old woman washing clothes in the icy water. Everyone called this washerwoman "Magpie" because of her constant chatter. "What are you girls doing out in this bitter cold?" she shouted hoarsely at them.

"But you are out, Mother," Bernadette answered, her voice tender with sympathy. Magpie was touched with her concern.

"If you are looking for wood," she advised, "you will find lots of branches in the Lafitte meadow. They were cutting trees there yesterday."

Bernadette thanked her but knew that they would never touch a stick without permission. Her upright spirit still bristled at the memory of Papa being hauled to jail for bringing home a discarded board. No, they would go to the public land along the Forest Road to pick up wood.

The girls ran through the meadow ignoring the dead branches of poplar and beech trees that lay all about, until they came to the shallow millstream which they had to cross to get to the Forest Road.

Across this stream was Massabielle, the "Old Hump," a rocky cliff. A cavern in the side of the cliff led into the depths of the hill. Strange stories were told of this dreary place. Some people even believed demons haunted it.

Bernadette sat on a rock to remove her stockings. Toinette and Baloum threw their shoes across the stream and stepped in cautiously. They held their heavy skirts high and shrieked when the cold water swirled around their feet and ankles.

"Toinette, Baloum," Bernadette called. "Wait a minute."

"Well, hurry up," demanded Baloum. "You are such a slowpoke, Bernie!"

"I am not," retorted Bernadette. "I have to take my stockings off." How she wished her mama would let her go barelegged like the other girls. She called to her sister, "Put some stones in the water, Toinette, so I can step over. There are some over there by the cave."

On the other side of the stream, Toinette began to haul stepping stones to the water for her sister. "Oh come on, Toinette!" Baloum said impatiently. "We'll be here all day if you do that. Let Bernie stay on the other side. We don't need her help anyway. We can collect lots of wood by ourselves."

When Toinette still hesitated, Baloum added, "Your father will beat you if we are gone for a long time." Toinette's gentle papa would never beat her, of course. Baloum just assumed he would act like her own fierce father.

Baloum ran ahead down the path. Toinette shrugged and waved goodbye to Bernadette. She hurried to catch up with her friend.

"No! Please wait for me," Bernadette cried, as she peeled off her stockings. "I'll be right there. I'm not afraid to wade across."

She did not like to see her sister going off alone with Baloum. Already she could hear them laughing and saw them flipping their skirts up about their knees. "Toinette," Bernadette shouted. "Keep your skirt down!"

The two friends soon disappeared around the bend, leaving Bernadette behind. "Baloum is bold and she swears," sighed Bernadette to herself. "But I can't protect Toinette from her anymore. I can't even keep up with my own little sister."

This last thought made her especially despondent. She and Toinette had always shared so much. Now Toinette was making new friends at school while Bernadette was still in the lowest class with the "babies" because she could barely read and write, although she was fourteen years old.

The catechism was so difficult that Bernadette wondered whether God even wanted her to learn. One day she asked her confessor about this, and Father Pomian answered, "God's ways are mysterious, child. You must be patient and do your best. He will let you know what He wants of you in due time."

Bernadette wondered whether "due time" would ever arrive. Her younger sister was already in the upper class and receiving communion every month. She would wear the white dress of a Child of Mary in the next procession while Bernadette could only watch from the sidelines.

Bernadette felt a little jealous of Toinette. She longed to be healthy like her sister. She worried about what she would do when she grew up. Looking up at the grey sky and the snow-covered mountains, she shivered and drew her cape over her arms. She thought of how cold the water in the millstream would be when she waded across. Bernadette was determined to catch up with the other two girls and do her share of carrying the wood home. Baloum's taunt, that they did not need her help, stuck in her heart like a thorn.

Bernadette was about to cross the stream when she heard the roar of wind as if a storm were coming. She looked around. "That's strange," she said to herself. "The wind is so strong, but the leaves are not moving."

Across the stream she could see the branches of a wild rose bush tossing and rattling against the rocky cliff. The plant seemed to be blown by wind that came from inside the cave—but surely that was impossible. Bernadette stared nervously at the cavern.

CHAPTER TEN

HEAVEN COMES TO EARTH

The wind died down. Then the niche in the rocks filled with golden light. Bernadette rubbed her eyes to make sure she was not dreaming. She rubbed them again, but the light still shone.

Glorious daylight seemed to be radiating from within the cavern. Bernadette was afraid at first. She kept gazing at the shining grotto, unable to move. Moments later a beautiful young woman appeared within the golden glow. Bernadette had never seen anyone as lovely as this Lady. She dropped to her knees, utterly captivated.

The exquisite Lady seemed barely older than Bernadette herself. She smiled, bowed and extended her arms towards Bernadette. The Lady's long white dress flowed down to her bare feet, each foot adorned by a light yellow rose. Her dress had full, wide sleeves and was drawn up around her neck with a cord. A sky-blue sash held it at the waist. A white veil covered the Lady's head and shoulders and fell to her feet, rippling in the slight breeze. Strands of hair peeked out from the veil at her temples. Gentle blue eyes lit up her oval face.

The Lady placed her hands palm to palm in prayer. A long white rosary on a yellow chain was draped over her arm. Bernadette quickly pulled her own little black rosary out of her pocket. She tried to lift her hand to make the Sign of the Cross but found she could not do so.

The Lady lifted the crucifix at the end of her own rosary and made the Sign of the Cross slowly and reverently. At that moment, Bernadette, too, could lift her hand. She made the Sign of the Cross just as the Lady had done. The Lady smiled in approval; then slipped her rosary beads through her fingers in time with Bernadette's prayers. The Lady's lips moved only when Bernadette said the "Glory to God" prayer at the end of each decade. Never had Bernadette prayed with so much fervor.

When the rosary was finished the Lady smiled, bowed once more and disappeared. The golden light gradually faded from the grotto. Bernadette remained on her knees, gazing in wonderment at the place where the Lady had stood.

The rude shouting of Baloum brought her back to her senses. "Hey, Bernie, you lazy fool! Why are you kneeling out here saying your prayers? You should be helping us!"

Jeanne and Toinette had returned; their arms loaded with twigs and branches of dead wood. Bernadette scrambled to her feet and waded across the stream toward them. "I thought you said this water was cold," she laughed. "It's as warm as dishwater."

Toinette and Baloum looked at each other, bewildered. What did Bernadette mean? To them, the water was ice cold.

"Did you see something, Bernadette?" asked Toinette. She knew it was not like her sister to get out of work by saying prayers, and wondered what had happened. Bernadette did not reply. Instead, she quickly picked up a load of wood, waded back through the stream, and ran lightly up the slope as if her wooden shoes had wings. The other two struggled along behind, amazed at her sudden strength and energy. When they sat down to rest at the top of the hill, Toinette begged her sister to tell them what she had seen.

"If I tell you, you must promise to keep it a secret," said Bernadette. She was now ready to tell them of her wonderful vision. The other two promised, crossing their hearts. Bernadette breathed deeply and began.

"In that big opening up on the rock I saw a golden light and a Lady appeared in the midst of it. She was very young, and lovely and gentle. She wore a long white dress and veil, and held a rosary made of large beads on a golden chain. She smiled at me all the time I was saying the rosary. I can't tell you how beautiful she was!"

The other girls were dumbfounded, unable to believe their ears. "Who was she?" asked Toinette finally.

"She did not speak to me," Bernadette answered. "But she was so delightful that I could have looked at her forever. When I finished my rosary, she disappeared."

Toinette and Baloum picked up their loads and hurried off. Bernadette followed slowly, savoring the memory of her wonderful vision.

Toinette forgot her promise to keep the secret and blurted out the news as soon as she got home. When Bernadette arrived, the whole family gathered around and demanded to know what she had seen. Bernadette joyfully answered all their questions.

To her surprise, Mama was furious. "What idiocy!" she shouted. "How can you make up stories about seeing the Blessed Virgin? That's a wicked thing to do."

"But Mama," Bernadette exclaimed, "I did not say it was the Blessed Virgin, only a beautiful Lady. And I did see her. I really did. Don't you believe me?"

Papa knew that Bernadette would not tell a deliberate lie, but he thought she imagined seeing a Lady. Or perhaps an evil spirit tricked her. "You will get us into trouble with this foolishness," he said. "You had better not go back to that place again!"

Bernadette's heart sank. Not go back?

"Oh, Papa," she begged. "Please, please let me go back. If I don't see her again, I think I shall die."

"Nonsense," said Papa. "Now you listen to me, my girl. I forbid you to go back to that place."

Bernadette's joy at seeing the radiant vision dissolved into dejection and inner turmoil. How could she obey her father and not go back? The young girl had not yet learned that the Lady could overcome any obstacle.

In the meantime, Baloum, who had no intention of keeping her promise, was busy telling the tale of Bernadette's Lady. Since it was market day in Lourdes, the story soon spread all over town and to the surrounding countryside. It was the subject of every conversation.

At the rectory, the priests chuckled at this childishness, except for Father Pomian, Bernadette's confessor, who knew her to be a sensible and honest girl. At the convent, the nuns were abuzz with the incredible story. In St. John's Club at the restaurant, the Café Français, the cynics sneered at this "superstitious nonsense."

In the homes of town and country folk, passionate discussions took place. They asked each other, "Who is this Bernadette? Could her story possibly be true?" Foolish imagination, most people agreed. Or perhaps the devil deceived the girl. Only a few thought Bernadette's vision might be real. The rest doubted or scoffed at the idea of a heavenly Lady appearing at Massabielle, which many believed was haunted. Besides, why should she appear to an ignorant little pauper like Bernadette Soubirous? It was impossible!

The police were suspicious. Was this a trick played by the priests and the Soubirous family to get money by fraud, they asked one another. They would have to keep a strict watch over that Soubirous girl. They were certainly not going to let anyone get away with stealing under the guise of religious revelations.

The early night of winter fell over the village. In the dungeon, the uneasy family slept fitfully. Bernadette, distressed that her parents did not believe her, pondered the events of that remarkable day. She wondered if she would ever see the beautiful Lady again.

CHAPTER ELEVEN

COME HERE
FOR A FORTNIGHT

Bernadette's teacher was indignant when she learned of her student's vision. "How dare that silly Soubirous girl claim she saw the Blessed Virgin?" thought the nun. "I'll put a stop to her preposterous story."

The next day, she made Bernadette stand in front of the class and tell what she had seen. When Bernadette described the Lady, her teacher realized the other children were fascinated. "That will be all, Bernadette," she interrupted crossly. "You may go back to your seat. We have heard enough of your ridiculous tale. Blessed Virgin, indeed. As if she would appear to you, and in such a place, fit only for pigs!"

"But, Sister, I did not say she was the Blessed Virgin," protested Bernadette.

"Silence!" her teacher commanded sharply. "How dare you answer me back! We will hear no more about this. I do not wish any of my pupils to discuss it."

Nevertheless, as soon as class was out, they gathered excitedly around Bernadette to listen to her story about the beautiful Lady. Bernadette gladly repeated all the details. She was dismayed when a few of the girls called her crazy, especially Baloum. Others were angry with her for "telling lies," as they said. One girl even slapped her face.

However, some of the school girls hoped to see the beautiful Lady, and urged Bernadette to beg permission to go back to the grotto. At first, Bernadette's parents flatly refused, but by Sunday, they began to relent.

"Perhaps it is someone holy, Louise," said Papa. "After all, the Lady did carry a rosary. Maybe we should let them go."

Mama agreed doubtfully. "They must take some holy water with them," she admonished. "If it is the devil playing a trick, he'll run away when Bernadette sprinkles holy water on the rock."

Their parents reluctantly allowed Bernadette and Toinette to go back to the grotto. Bernadette first ran to get holy water from the church. She and her sister then set off by the short route, over the hill. A few other girls tagged along, curious to get a glimpse of the Lady. Baloum straggled behind and waited at the top of the hill where she could watch what happened.

When they arrived in front of the grotto, Bernadette told them to kneel with her and say the rosary. Soon the miraculous light appeared and, to Bernadette's joy, the beautiful Lady stood before her in the niche once more. Though the Lady smiled warmly at all the girls, only Bernadette could see her. Bernadette then sprinkled her holy water toward the grotto; the Lady smiled and came even closer.

The other girls were startled by a loud bang. Baloum had tossed a large rock from above that hit the boulder on which Bernadette was leaning. Bernadette did not even notice. Her heart and soul were caught up in the heavenly vision and she was unaware of what was happening around her.

Bernadette's face was pale and lit by a strange radiance. She was so still that some of the girls panicked. "You have killed Bernadette," they shouted at Baloum, who was scampering down the hill.

"That's silly," Baloum retorted. "If she were dead she would fall over, not be kneeling up like that."

The frantic group began to shout at Bernadette and to shake her, but they could not break her trance. Bernadette's eyes remained uplifted to the niche in the rock; her face shining with joy. She sometimes smiled, at other times tears rolled down her cheeks. A few of the girls began to cry. One of them ran over to the Savy Mill nearby, and fetched the miller, Antoine Nicolau, and his mother.

Antoine was a strong young man, but he and Mrs. Nicolau could barely lift Bernadette to her feet and drag her, struggling, along the path to their house. The girl remained in her ecstasy, looking up toward the sky, for the Lady followed her. Bernadette's face was glowing until they arrived at the millhouse. Then the Lady disappeared.

When Bernadette became aware of her surroundings, she found herself seated in the Nicolau's kitchen in the midst of an excited crowd of women from the town. Her mama stood in front of the group, waving a stick. "You little rogue," she cried. "What do you mean by making everyone run after you?"

"But Mama," Bernadette replied, "I never told anyone to come with me."

Fearful that Bernadette's strange behavior would make a laughing stock of the family, her mama lifted her stick to beat her daughter. Mrs. Nicolau stopped her. "What are you doing, Louise?" she gasped. "You must not strike your daughter. She is an angel."

Antoine agreed. "In all my life," he reported later, "I have never seen anything as lovely as that girl's face when she was praying at the grotto."

The others then described to Bernadette how pale and extraordinary she looked while she was seeing the Lady. They told her about the scare they had when Baloum's rock hit the boulder, and about how she did not react to anything around her. For her part, Bernadette described the Lady to the people gathered around. She answered most of their probing questions.

Although the others were intrigued, her mama and papa did not believe Bernadette had really seen a heavenly Lady. They thought this foolishness had gone far enough. They flatly refused to let her visit the grotto again, although she tearfully begged for permission.

Later that day, however, Mrs. Millet, her mama's employer, convinced them to allow Bernadette to go back. She hoped the Lady might be her own daughter, who had died recently. She believed her dead child might now be in Purgatory and that her ghost might be appearing to ask for prayers. Was not the Lady dressed in blue and white, as her daughter had been when she was president of the Children of Mary?

"My sewing woman and I will go with Bernadette very early in the morning," Mrs. Millet told Louise. "That way no one will follow and we can find out who the Lady is." Then she added, "And we will take some paper and a pen, and ask the Lady to write down her name."

Bernadette's mama felt obliged to agree. She could not deny a request from her employer.

Before dawn the next morning, Mrs. Millet and her servant were kneeling with Bernadette in front of the grotto. The Lady once more appeared in her aura of golden light. After praying the rosary, Bernadette approached and held the pen and paper toward the Lady as Madame Millet requested.

"Please, my Lady, would you kindly write down your name and what you wish from me?" she asked politely.

The Lady laughed, and Bernadette heard her gentle voice for the first time. "There is no need to write down what I have to say to you," she said. The Lady spoke in Bernadette's native dialect, used only by the people in Bigorre, the province of France where the Soubirous lived. Then she added, "Will you do me the favor of coming here every day for a fortnight?"

"I will come if my parents give me permission," Bernadette replied, astonished that the Lady would address her so respectfully in her own native tongue, not the Parisian French that the girl found so difficult.

This pleased her heavenly visitor, who then said, "I cannot promise to make you happy in this world, but in the next." Then she disappeared.

Mrs. Millet was disappointed because she and her companion had neither seen nor heard the Lady. On their way home, Mrs. Millet cautioned, "Beware, Bernadette! If you are telling lies, God will punish you."

In spite of their doubts, the two women persuaded Bernadette's parents to let the girl return to the grotto each day for fourteen days, as the Lady requested. Mrs. Millet also offered to keep Bernadette at her own house. She pointed out to Louise that this would relieve the disruption to the Soubirous family caused by the many pilgrims who followed Bernadette right into the dungeon.

The Millets welcomed Bernadette to their mansion. They gave her a lovely dress to wear and had their servants wait on her. Yet, the girl stayed with them for only a few nights. Her Papa and Mama decided they wanted Bernadette to live at home, and their daughter quietly complied.

The next market day, the town of Lourdes overflowed with people. Carriages arrived loaded with pilgrims and curious tourists. Everyone, it seemed, wanted to go to Massabielle. "Have you heard that the Blessed Virgin is supposed to have appeared to Bernadette Soubirous?" one said to another.

The crowd at the cave by the river alarmed the police. It was their duty to keep order in the town. Although the onlookers had been peaceful and prayerful, one never knew when trouble would start. Police and soldiers at the castle barracks stayed on the alert. They watched Bernadette's comings and goings and examined the entire grotto carefully.

So far, the clergy had not said anything about Bernadette or the apparitions. The civic authorities had taken no action either. But that was soon to change. Pilgrims were arriving in Lourdes in ever greater numbers and the authorities wanted to nip this problem in the bud. They decided to bring Bernadette in for questioning.

After Vespers the following Sunday evening, a constable came to take "that Soubirous girl" to the office of Mr. Jacomet, the Police Commissioner. The constable marched up to the church and, in the sight of all, seized Bernadette and hauled her toward police headquarters. Bernadette teased the policeman.

"Hold my arm tight. I might escape!"

Chapter Twelve

The Police Interrogate Bernadette

The Police Commissioner, Mr. Jacomet, sat behind the polished desk of his stylish office. Winter light filtered through the silk drapes and fine lace curtains on the tall narrow windows. It reflected on shelves of leather-bound books. Ornately carved chairs, upholstered in red velvet, were arranged along the walls. Bernadette stepped lightly over the large Oriental rug and stood before the officer's desk.

Mr. Jacomet was handsome and imposing. His uniform was spotless and tailored to fit him perfectly. The officer's manner in ordinary life was gentlemanly; he got along well with his fellow parishioners at St. Peter's Church. Bernadette had often seen him speaking to Father Peyramale after Mass. However, he was now on duty as a police investigator and treated the young girl as if she were suspected of a crime. He did not ask her to sit down but immediately began to interrogate her. He dipped his pen into the ink pot, ready to write down her answers.

"Your name?" he asked brusquely.

"But Mr. Jacomet, you know my name," replied Bernadette.

"Answer the question! Your name, please."

"Bernadette Soubirous."

After writing down her name and address, Mr. Jacomet asked her about the Lady, demanding to know all the details of how Bernadette had first seen her, what she wore, and what she said.

Bernadette described the Lady exactly. The Police Commissioner wrote down her answers. Then he read his notes back to her, deliberately making mistakes to entrap Bernadette into contradicting herself. This was one of his favorite tricks, which he used to confuse suspects whom he assumed were telling lies. He did not believe that Bernadette had really seen a heavenly vision and suspected her of fabricating this fantastic story to attract money from pious or superstitious people.

"You say the Lady wore a blue dress with a white sash."

"No, Mr. Jacomet, a white dress with a blue sash. You must have written it down wrong," Bernadette replied calmly.

"Mmm. And you say her hair hung down her back."

"No, sir. It was her veil that hung down her back."

On and on the questioning went for two hours while Bernadette remained in front of his desk, demure in her Sunday best: a clean blouse and shawl, with a blue and white striped kerchief tied around her head in the Pyrenean way. The girl's clear brown eyes were steady and attentive as she listened to Mr. Jacomet's questions. Not once did she waver in her answers or in her steady, polite manner. Mr. Jacomet was not able to confuse her or catch her in any lies.

The officer could hear the angry murmuring of a group of townspeople that had gathered below his window, waiting for Bernadette to be released. Mr. Jacomet became nervous and exasperated. This was not going as he expected. His hand was shaking so much that he had trouble dipping his pen into the inkwell.

"Are you willing to promise never to go to Massabielle again?" he finally bellowed.

"But sir, I have promised to go there every day for a fortnight."

The policeman lost his self-control. "You mean to go again? Then I'll send for the guards. Get ready to go to prison."

"So much the better," Bernadette replied fearlessly. "I shall cost my father less, and in prison you'll come and teach me my catechism."

Just then, Bernadette's father burst into the office. He was afraid of the police, especially since they had put him in prison for taking home a board he had found on the street. He was worried that the police might jail Bernadette.

Mr. Jacomet greeted him impatiently. "Who are you, and what do you mean by barging into my office?"

"I am the father of this child," declared François. "I have come for my daughter. She has done nothing wrong."

"She may go," retorted Mr. Jacomet sternly. "But I have told her not to return to Massabielle. She is underage and you are responsible for her. See that she obeys my orders."

"Yes, sir," Bernadette's papa agreed readily. "That is what I want. I will remind her of what you said."

Mr. Jacomet was very relieved that Bernadette's father had come to get her. He had feared the angry crowd might break in and take the girl by force. Leaning back on his chair, the flustered officer reassured himself that now the excitement would blow over. The commissioner was so confident that François would not dare to let his daughter return to the grotto that he made a big blunder. He released a false version of the interview with Bernadette to the journalists.

Up to that time, the newspapers had not carried any news of the events at Massabielle. The next day, however, the headlines blared:

"HOAX EXPOSED"

"VIRGIN OF THE GROTTO A FRAUD"

Long accounts boasted about how the police had halted the whole affair. Newspapers all over France and even in other countries printed this news. Editors called for public authorities to board up the grotto, and to forcibly end the "religious scam."

In spite of the uproar and publicity, the police did not dare to bar pilgrims from the place. Increasing numbers of people visited Massabielle every day, even when Bernadette was not there. Some spent whole nights at the grotto in prayer, their candles glimmering against the rocks. Mr. Jacomet found no excuse to halt these activities since the pilgrims were always peaceful.

CHAPTER THIRTEEN

A MIRACULOUS SPRING

Bernadette's feet dragged on her way to school the next morning. Her encounter with the police had terrified her parents, and they forbade her to go to the grotto or even to morning Mass. Dejectedly, she climbed the marble steps of the imposing schoolhouse and passed through the enormous colonnade. She was late, but it did not seem important that day.

As she opened the heavy door, she gave a start of surprise. A furious Mother Superior, directress of the whole convent, awaited her in the large entrance hall. Bernadette gazed timidly at the formidable nun in her long black habit and white coif. She feared the Sisters would be upset about her being questioned by the police, but Mother Superior's anger and sarcasm stunned her.

"Well, little Miss, have you finished with your carnival capers?" she taunted. "This is the first time that a student of our convent has been arrested by the police. You have brought shame and disgrace on our school and your fellow students. If you would settle down and learn your catechism instead of running around after false visions, we would all be much better off. Get to your class and don't let me hear another word about this nonsense."

With these words, she turned her back on Bernadette and swept out of the foyer.

News of Mother Superior's rebuke buzzed through the school. Some of the other pupils were not slow to show their spite. At lunchtime they collected around her, jeering, "Bernadette's going to jail, going to jail. Serves her right, serves her right."

Bernadette's friends hung back. Some looked at her with suspicion. Others sympathized, but feared being mocked along with her. Bernadette felt ostracized. Yet what distressed her most was that her parents refused to let her go back to the grotto. The previous evening she had pleaded with them, to no avail.

"Mama, you already gave me permission to go and I promised the Lady. Please let me. Oh, if you could just see her, Mama, you would surely let me go. She is so beautiful."

Mama turned her face away. Papa simply repeated, "The police have forbidden it. Do you want us all to go to jail?"

Bernadette had always obeyed her parents. But now she felt a higher call to obedience that she knew she must not resist. The next day, Bernadette once more knelt at the entrance of the cave. When her beloved Lady appeared, she told Bernadette that she wanted to give her some secrets. She asked the young girl to promise never to tell anyone what they were, no matter who asked. She also taught her a special prayer to say each day.

Bernadette solemnly promised never to reveal the secrets. She said the words of the special prayer silently every day, just as they had come from the Lady's own lips, and she held the secrets in her heart for the rest of her life.

The following day, Bernadette received the first message she was to give to the people. At one point she turned to the crowd, lifted her arms wide, and, imitating the gestures she had seen in her vision, she cried out loudly, "Penance. Penance. Penance."

Some in the crowd wept, feeling the reproach of the heavenly visitor. This message touched so many hearts that immediately afterwards, the churches filled with penitents who wanted to confess their sins to the priests and receive God's forgiveness.

At the next apparition, however, Bernadette's actions shocked everyone. What she did seemed so bizarre that most onlookers thought she had gone insane. During the vision, Bernadette crawled back and forth in front of the cavern on her knees. She dug with her hands in a moist patch in the sandy ground. After lifting out several handfuls of ooze, she put some of the muddy water into her mouth, and smeared it on her face. Then, still on her knees, she reached up and ate some grass growing on the slope. When she completed these tasks and turned back to the grotto, the Lady had disappeared.

Bernadette came out of her ecstasy to find her Aunt Bernarde wiping mud off her face. People were shouting, "The girl's gone crazy. She's a madwoman." Some even threw stones. If the police had not protected her, Bernadette might have been injured. Sickened and disgusted, most of the crowd left the grotto—forever, as they thought.

Bernadette's aunt led her home to her family. When they asked her why she had behaved in this strange way, she explained, "The Lady told me to look for a spring, to drink the water in it, to wash in it and to eat some of the grass there. At first, the water was too muddy to drink, but it became clearer as I dug in it, and then I drank and washed. I picked some grass. I chewed it, but it tasted so nasty that I spit it out."

This story filled Bernadette's parents with concern and fear, especially when they heard how the crowd had hissed and shouted insults at their young daughter. "Next time Papa will be with you, my girl," he assured her. "Let the police arrest me if they dare. I know now that the Lady really comes to you and she will look after us." Mama also promised to go with her.

While Bernadette's family was engaged in this discussion, astonishing events were taking place at the grotto.

Although most of the assembled people had stormed off in angry disillusionment, a few remained in front of the niche, weeping for Bernadette and for the loss of their sweet hopes. Among them was Antoine Nicolau, who noticed that water was streaming out of the place where Bernadette had dug in the mud.

"Come back! Come back!" he shouted to the departing stragglers. "Look, a spring. The Lady has sent us a spring."

Some of the people rushed back. In joy and amazement, they drank the fresh pure water that flowed in greater and greater abundance. That very day, Antoine and many of his fellow-stone masons began to build a basin to hold the water from the miraculous spring.

Remarkable healings occurred in several people who touched or drank the water. A dying baby revived. A blind man recovered his sight. People who had lost their faith returned to God. Those who had mocked the church confessed their sins to the priest, and attended Mass. Slowly the presence of the gentle, beautiful Lady permeated the whole valley.

Chapter Fourteen
Build a Chapel

Bernadette had to push her way through the throng to her place in front of the grotto. People throughout the region had learned of the marvelous spring with its healing power, and wanted to see for themselves. The crowd extended over the meadow and even to the hills on the other side of the Gave River. In spite of the bitter February weather, many had waited for most of the night, eager to see Bernadette in ecstasy as she spoke to the Lady from heaven.

When Bernadette knelt to say the rosary, the pilgrims brought out their own rosaries. The murmur of prayer arose from all sides: "Hail Mary, full of grace…."

Once more Bernadette's face shone with a heavenly radiance as the Lady appeared and talked to her. Again the Lady asked her to crawl around the grotto on her hands and knees and to kiss the ground, as penance for sinners. She asked her to drink from the spring and wash in it. This time the crowd was prayerful, and did not jeer.

When Bernadette came out of her ecstasy, she told her Aunt Bernarde that the Lady had asked her to go to the priests and tell them that she wished to have a chapel built at the place where she appeared.

Her aunt advised her goddaughter to give the Lady's message to Father Pomian, because he was gentle and approachable. So Bernadette told her confessor about the Lady's request for the chapel. To her chagrin, he insisted that she give the message in person to the pastor, Father Peyramale.

Many people were afraid of Father Peyramale. His outbursts of temper intimidated parishioners. Bernadette shrank back at the thought of talking to the hot-tempered priest—but Aunt Bernarde shrank back even more. She absolutely refused to face Father Peyramale. So Bernadette persuaded her young Aunt Basile to accompany her to the rectory.

In spite of the cold weather, Bernadette and Aunt Basile found the pastor in his garden, pacing back and forth. He wore a large black overcoat, a scarf around his neck, and a woolen hat pulled over his ears. He was reading prayers from his breviary. Annoyed at the intrusion, he glared at the two girls.

"What do you want? Well, get on with it."

Swallowing hard and bowing politely, Bernadette replied, "Please, Father, I have come to bring you a message from the Lady. She wants a chapel built at Massabielle."

"Lady?" the priest asked, as if surprised. "I know of no Lady. Who is she?"

"She is the Lady who appears to me at the grotto. She is very beautiful and is surrounded with light," Bernadette replied, amazed that he did not know what everyone else knew.

"Mmm. What is her name?"

"I do not know, Father. I have asked her but she does not tell me; she just smiles."

"Surely you cannot expect me to build a chapel for a Lady who won't say who she is! Besides, I haven't any money. Have you?"

"No, Father."

"Very strange. She wants me to build a chapel without any money but she will not even tell us her name. Now, you go back to the grotto and ask the Lady who she is and where we can get the money for a chapel. Then when we know that, we will think about it. Is that fair?"

Bernadette knew he did not believe she had seen the Lady. Nevertheless, she bowed and replied simply, "Yes, Father, I will ask her."

The townspeople soon learned that the Lady wanted a chapel. Many people, both rich and poor, offered the pastor money to help build it, but he refused to accept any. He informed them crossly that they ought to set up a fund for the poor instead.

Although some of Father Peyramale's most faithful parishioners told him of the miraculous healings at the new spring, the priest thought the girl was living in a fantasy world. He knew there were crackpots who claimed to see God or the Blessed Virgin. Before going to the grotto himself, and thereby implying the church's approval, he wanted to be solidly convinced that her vision was holy and of God, and that Bernadette was not being deceived. Father Peyramale, therefore, would not visit the grotto and forbade the other priests in the parish from going there.

Every time the Lady appeared, she asked again for a chapel. She also said that there should be candlelight processions to the grotto. Bernadette brought each request to Father Peyramale. This took all her courage, for the pastor was getting more and more annoyed.

"Well, once again, what is this Lady's name?" he shouted.

"I don't know, Father. She does not wish to give her name."

"Well then, since she does not wish to give her name, you are a liar. It's scandalous! How do you expect us to organize a procession for this Lady? Maybe we should give you a torch all to yourself, and you can run your own procession. You have plenty of followers; you've no need of priests."

"I never say anything to anyone. I do not ask them to come with me," Bernadette answered bravely.

Aunt Basile heard how harshly he spoke to her. "It made me shudder to listen to him," she admitted later. "It made me shrivel up to nothing."

Bernadette tolerated the storm of Father Peyramale's ridicule, just as she had endured the long questioning of Police Commissioner Jacomet. She was determined to carry out the Lady's requests at any cost.

Even though the police wanted to close up the grotto, they had no excuse because the crowds were on public land and gave them no trouble. Neither could the police catch any of the Soubirous family taking money from the pilgrims, though they watched very closely. Commissioner Jacomet sent local constables to keep their eyes on Bernadette and her family. They even peeked in their little window to make sure that the family was not taking gifts from the hundreds of people who pushed into their cellar room each day to glimpse Bernadette.

People did offer money and gifts to the Soubirous family, but they would not take anything. Against his family's wishes, Johnny once dared to accept a few pennies as payment for leading a group of out-of-town pilgrims to Massabielle. This angered Bernadette so much that she boxed his ears and made him give the money back.

The police were also concerned about safety at the site. People climbed trees to get a better view of the grotto, they hung from the top of the rock, and they knelt, wedged into every possible spot. Yet, there were no accidents.

"The greatest miracle at Lourdes is that no one has been killed," said Police Chief Jacomet. In spite of his strong misgivings, the officer was unable to find a reason to forbid the gatherings, for the people were devout and peaceful, and most believed in the Lady even though they could not see her.

The reverent spirit of the place even influenced the police and the soldiers sent to keep order at the grotto. They commanded the throng to make way for Bernadette when she arrived. In full uniform, glistening with brass buttons and gold braid, they marched beside her through the crowd as if they were her guard of honor. One constable even ordered the people to kiss the ground when Bernadette did, and he did the same. All the soldiers knelt down with the rest of the pilgrims. The Lady was winning many hearts.

Still, some authorities in the church and the government were derisive. The newspapers continued to make fun of her. Doctors from Paris examined her to see if she had a nervous disease, but they could find nothing wrong. Scientists tested the water of the spring to find out why it cured people, but their tests showed ordinary spring water, pure and safe to drink. Everything possible was done to discover whether the apparitions were due to delusion or fraud.

All this testing and the doubts of the skeptics meant nothing to Bernadette. She only wanted to keep her promises to the beautiful Lady. The heavenly one had asked her to come to the grotto each day for fourteen days, and had appeared almost every day.

The last day of the fortnight arrived. It was a Thursday—market day. The usually bustling market was almost deserted because most of the townspeople were at Massabielle. About eight thousand people crowded around the grotto, eager to learn the Lady's name. They were certain this day would be the climax and the Lady would tell Bernadette who she was.

Everyone was disappointed. The Lady appeared and talked to Bernadette for a long time, but she did not reveal her name. Bernadette went home in sorrow. She was grief-stricken that the fortnight of visits was over and yet the Lady had withheld her name.

Although Bernadette did not return to the grotto for the next three weeks, the crowds kept coming. Water from the spring, "Lourdes Water," was carried all over the world. Miraculous healings continued to occur. Bernadette waited with longing for the Lady's gentle voice in her heart that would summon her to the grotto once more.

CHAPTER FIFTEEN

I AM THE IMMACULATE CONCEPTION

Bernadette was certain she had failed the Lady. The priests turned a deaf ear to her plea to build a chapel at Massabielle and to have processions. "Why wouldn't the Lady tell me her name?" thought Bernadette woefully. "I must have done something to offend her."

The girl continued to go to school and to study her spelling book and catechism. Progress was slow, even with the private teaching of her nun mentor. Toinette, who used to be her close companion, ran away impatiently when Bernadette asked for help. Toinette did not care much for books. More than that, Bernadette could see that her sister had become almost a stranger to her, both because of her own extraordinary visions and because of Toinette's new friendships.

Although she keenly missed the special closeness with her sister, Bernadette suffered this pain in her heart silently, for the conversion of sinners, as the Lady had taught her to do.

She now had a room of her own for the first time in her life. The Soubirous' landlord, André Sajous, who lived in the apartment upstairs, believed in Bernadette's visions from the start. He and his family now allowed her to occupy a room in their home. There she could receive her numerous visitors without disturbing her family. She could also study and pray and prepare for her First Communion, which was to occur on June 3rd.

So many pilgrims to Lourdes went to visit Bernadette that sometimes the police had to enter the house and establish two-way traffic lines going up and down the stairs. Bernadette answered all questions patiently and politely, repeating the same answers over and over again.

The Soubirous family continued to staunchly refuse the numerous donations offered by compassionate visitors. Bernadette also declined to bless people's rosaries. "Go to the priest if you want your rosary blessed," she would say.

The Commissioner of Police Jacomet was greatly relieved when the fortnight of apparitions was over. However, he ordered the local constables to continue to keep watch on Bernadette's family to make sure they were not accepting money. The secular newspapers crowed about Bernadette's failure to find out the name of the Lady or to get a chapel built. The cynical gentlemen who drank their morning coffee in the Café Français sneered that religion was once again shown to be a fraud.

Nevertheless, the "affair of Massabielle" was far from over. Crowds flooded into Lourdes from all over the province, from all over France and even from other countries. Some came out of devotion or hoping for a healing. Others came out of curiosity. A few came to scoff and jeer.

The believers who gathered at the shrine had no doubt that the water gushing from the spring at Lourdes was miraculous. Hundreds of sick people, whom medical doctors diagnosed as incurable, were brought to the grotto. Some were healed of even the most severe diseases.

Among the first to experience a remarkable cure was Louis Bouriette, a stonemason in Lourdes. His right eye was blind as a result of a mine explosion twenty years before. One day his daughter brought home water from the spring. When her father washed the blind eye in the water, his sight was instantly restored. Full of joy, he went around the town, shouting, "I can see! I can see!" to all who would listen.

Dr. Dozous tested Louis Bouriette's eyes and made certain that the sight of both was perfect, although the scar from the injury remained on the right eye. The doctor could find no natural reason for the man's restored vision.

News of these marvelous cures spread far and wide, causing hopeful pilgrims to pour into Lourdes. Many were healed, physically and spiritually. The grotto had become a shrine. A statue of the Blessed Virgin was placed in an arbor decorated with flowers, and candles burned continuously on the altar.

Bernadette's visions were the talk of the countryside. Many people believed, but others wondered if the miracles performed at the spring were just a trick or the result of mass hysteria. In homes, work places and schools, people vigorously argued about these questions.

One day, the magistrate, Judge Ribes, summoned Bernadette to the court of the tribunal for questioning. To people in the town, this was almost as bad as being sent to jail.

Bernadette, however, was willing to give witness to the message of the Lady. The formal atmosphere of the large, high-ceilinged court did not overwhelm her. She serenely observed the large picture of Emperor Napoleon III on the wall, the jury box and witness stand, the railing that separated the audience from the judge, and the dais where the judge sat on his ornate chair. She noticed the bearded lawyers and court officials in black frock coats and beige trousers as they hurried to and fro with sheaves of paper.

From behind the railing, little Bernadette gazed up at the examining magistrate in his official robes. He looked at the girl severely over his spectacles while he questioned her.

"I hear this so-called Lady asked you to behave like an animal, eating grass," he said, to provoke her.

Bernadette's quick wit did not fail. "Do we act like animals when we eat salad?" she responded.

The magistrate kept Bernadette standing in the court for most of the afternoon, answering his gruff questions about her visions. He finally had to admit that she repeated her story sensibly and accurately. She gave no sign of weariness or the ache she felt because he doubted her honesty.

Continual attacks could not break Bernadette's spirit, for she felt the presence of the Holy Spirit giving her the courage to stand up to the suspicious enquiries of the civic authorities. Like others who had questioned Bernadette, Judge Ribes was impressed by her clear answers, her simplicity and her innocence. He did not find any reason to arrest her.

Police Commissioner Jacomet wrote regular reports to Baron Massy, the county Prefect, about the events at Lourdes. The Prefect, in turn, reported to the Minister of Public Worship in Paris. These prominent men were furious at this outpouring of popular piety. They wanted the regional soldiers to shut down the whole business.

Mr. Jacomet pulled at his elegant moustache worriedly. He paced up and down over his fine carpet. He would dearly like to please his superiors and oust the pilgrims overflowing the town. But how was he to do it? "Even a dike of gendarmes could not hold back such a flood," he muttered to his clerk. "But at least the Soubirous girl does not go to the grotto now. Perhaps it will soon blow over." He could not have been more mistaken.

Spring flowers were blooming when Bernadette felt an inner call to return to the grotto. She persuaded Lucile, her young aunt, to accompany her and to bring a large, blessed candle. In her eagerness, Bernadette was soon running far ahead of her companion. She reached the top of the great hill and bounded down the other side, keeping her balance by catching onto small bushes with their newly sprouted leaves.

Although Bernadette told nobody she was coming to the grotto, a large crowd had spent the night there. They were hoping the Lady might appear that day because it was March 25, the Feast of the Annunciation. This day celebrates the Angel Gabriel appearing to Mary in Nazareth and inviting her to become the mother of Jesus, the Savior of the world. The pilgrims hoped the Lady would appear on her own special feast day. They were not disappointed.

When Bernadette arrived, the first rays of dawn lit up the clear sky. The Lady was waiting for her, clothed in her exquisite white dress and veil, her sash as soft and blue as the sky itself. It seemed to Bernadette that this dress must have been woven by angels. The Lady was smiling at the crowd the way a fond mother smiles at her children.

When Bernadette knelt in her place in front of the grotto, the Lady moved down from her niche to the entrance of the cave. Enraptured, Bernadette arose and stood in front of her, holding her candle and her rosary beads.

"Oh, my Lady, will you kindly tell me your name?" she implored. "The priests will not build a chapel or allow processions until they know who you are." The Lady smiled and bowed but said nothing.

Twice more Bernadette repeated her plea. After the third time, she received her answer. Opening her arms, the Lady looked out at the crowd. She joined her hands, palm to palm, lifted her eyes to heaven and said, "I am the Immaculate Conception."

Then she smiled lovingly at Bernadette, and disappeared. When Bernadette came out of her ecstasy, her family and friends surrounded her. "What did she say? Did she give her name?" they asked.

Bernadette was laughing with joy when she told them the Lady's name. Then she rushed off to tell Father Peyramale, repeating the words all the way, in case she might make a mistake. Bernadette and her Aunt Lucile rushed into the rectory. In their excitement, they forgot to knock or even to greet the pastor respectfully.

"I am the Immaculate Conception," Bernadette blurted out to him.

At first, the startled priest did not understand what they were trying to tell him.

"It's the Lady's name!" exclaimed Bernadette. "She told me that she is the Immaculate Conception."

Father Peyramale was astounded. He knew that this was one of the names of the Blessed Virgin Mary, which the Pope had proclaimed only a few years before, in December 1854. Most Catholics had not yet heard this name for the Blessed Mother. Surely, Bernadette could not be making this up.

"Do you know what the Immaculate Conception means?" he asked.

Bernadette said she did not know.

"It means," he said slowly, "that the Lady who is appearing to you is the Blessed Virgin." He staggered back to his chair, his massive form trembling with emotion. "Mary has this title because she was conceived in her mother's womb without the stain of

Original Sin," he explained in an awed voice. "It tells us that she was full of God's grace from the first moment of her existence."

Recovering from his emotion, he said in his usual curt manner, "You may both leave now. I have to think this over. I shall consider what is to be done."

Bernadette and Aunt Lucile left, bowing respectfully. Bernadette did not think it was the right time to mention a chapel and processions again. That would come, she was now sure. She hurried home to share the glorious news with her family and friends.

Chapter Sixteen

The Authorities Versus the Lady

The news flashed all over France. "The Lady of Lourdes gave her name. She is the Immaculate Conception, the Blessed Virgin herself!"

The news went by couriers on horseback, by telegraph and by mail to Baron Massy, to Bishop Laurence at Tarbes, to the Minister of Public Worship in Paris, and to convents and newspapers all over the world. Much against her wishes, Bernadette found herself a celebrity. Photos of her were being sold for a few cents in the marketplace.

The reaction was an enormous wave of thanksgiving and a revival of faith among Catholics in France. At the grotto, votive offerings, such as pictures and tablets, gave witness to cures of the deaf, the blind and the lame. Testimonies of doctors who vouched for these healings were carefully preserved.

A well-known writer, Henri Lasserre, was healed of "physical and moral blindness" and restored to a fervent faith in Christ and in the Catholic Church. In thanksgiving for his healing, he wrote two books on the history of the pilgrimages and miracles of Lourdes.

These books, translated into many languages, extended the fame of Lourdes throughout the world.

He wrote about the miraculous healing of a workman, Autun, who thought that religion was only for women. While Autun was still quite young, tumors and ulcers in his legs crippled him. After much suffering, he was desperate and allowed his devout wife to bathe him with water from Lourdes. His legs were healed completely. His heart was converted and he came to believe in and love God.

Dr. Dozous of Lourdes, who had known Bernadette since she was a child and cared for her when she almost died with cholera, had already witnessed healings. Yet, he was not completely convinced of the truth of her visions. Although the doctor was not a fervent Catholic, he had a brilliant mind and an open heart. When the men at the Café Français scoffed at the miracles, he would stroke his beard and comment that, in his experience, Bernadette was sincere and well-balanced, and not the type to imagine things or to tell lies.

His remaining skepticism finally dissolved during the seventeenth apparition, on April 7, almost two weeks after the Lady revealed her name. It was the second-to-last time that Bernadette saw the Lady.

Dr. Dozous took a place beside Bernadette during this vision. While she was in ecstasy, he noticed that her large blessed candle slipped down so that the flame licked her fingers and hand. The crowd cried out in alarm. Johnny tried to snatch the candle away, but Dr. Dozous prevented him. Although the flame engulfed her hand for several minutes, Bernadette was enraptured and did not feel it. Dr. Dozous held her wrist and found her pulse steady and her breathing calm. When Bernadette came out of her ecstasy, she immediately dropped the candle and the flame went out.

The doctor asked her gently, "May I look at your hand?" She willingly held it out to him. He stared in amazement. There were no blisters or burn marks whatsoever. "There are no burns on her hand," he shouted to the crowd. "There is nothing."

Then Dr. Dozous picked up the candle, relit it, and pushed the flame under Bernadette's hand. She drew away quickly, exclaiming, "You're burning me!"

The "Miracle of the Candle" became widely known. From that time, Dr. Dozous believed Bernadette really did see a heavenly Lady. Thereafter, the doctor tried to persuade other scientists to investigate the reality of the miracles, but the French Academy of Science refused to even consider them.

One of the greatest moments in Bernadette's life occurred just a few weeks later. On June 3, 1858, she made her First Communion in the nun's chapel on the Feast of Corpus Christi. At long last, Bernadette could join in the procession, wearing her white dress and cape, with a lace veil over her long brown hair. Sister Victorine, her nun mentor, and Father Pomian had worked hard to teach her the catechism answers in French. They agreed she understood her religion and readily gave their permission for her to approach the altar rail at Mass and receive Jesus in the form of the holy Host.

Much later, when someone asked which made her happier—to see the Blessed Lady or to go to Communion—Bernadette replied, "I don't know. These two things go together; I can't compare them. All I know is that I was intensely happy in both cases."

About the same time that Bernadette was in church making her First Communion, Dr. Dozous witnessed another miracle at the grotto. Among the crowd of more than four thousand people, Dr. Dozous noticed a peasant couple carrying a boy about five years old, who could not walk.

The doctor asked the parents to allow him to examine the boy. After he diagnosed the child's medical condition as paralysis of the spine, Dr. Dozous helped to bathe him in the spring water. When the youngster was dressed and placed on the ground, he ran to his parents who, according to the doctor, "smothered him with vigorous hugs, shedding tears of joy." From that day, the boy could walk and play like other children.

Such miraculous healings did not impress the authorities. Baron Massy, the Regional Prefect, was determined to put an end to the pilgrimages to the Lourdes grotto. He was a man of great power and influence. He sent orders to Police Commissioner Jacomet and to Mayor Lacadé to arrest Bernadette secretly the next time she went to the grotto. They were to immediately transport her to Tarbes and confine her in the insane asylum there.

Although the doctors who examined Bernadette did not agree that she belonged in a mental hospital, the Baron knew that this was the only way to get rid of her. Then he would have the shrine boarded up and that would be the end of the Lourdes affair, he thought.

Word of the Baron's orders soon spread through the town of Lourdes. "They are going to send Bernadette to the crazy house!"

For the first time, Bernadette was terrified. She had heard stories about the horrific conditions in that asylum. Her worst nightmare was coming true. She prayed, and suddenly received an answer. She must take refuge with Father Peyramale. As the pastor, he had the authority to protect her. She ran to his house, breathless with fear. Father Peyramale assured her that he would save her from harm.

When Mayor Lacadé received orders from the Baron to arrest Bernadette, he was sure he could get the sanction of the Church through his friend, Father Peyramale. He and Police Commissioner Jacomet called on the pastor to enlist his support. They did not receive the warm welcome they expected.

Father Peyramale had been completely won over by Bernadette's courage and sincerity. Ever since the Lady revealed her name, he believed that his young parishioner had indeed seen the Blessed Virgin Mary. The thought of the innocent child being imprisoned in the dreadful asylum in Tarbes kindled his enormous temper. "Gentlemen," thundered the priest to the two officials, "Bernadette is not insane. She is causing no disorder. She is not a danger to herself or to others. Her family may be poor, but understand this: she is not alone! Kindly tell Baron Massy to send his soldiers if he wishes. They will have to pass over my dead body before they touch a hair on the head of that girl."

Father Peyramale had once driven wolves out of his garden. He now drove off the human wolves who wished to destroy Bernadette. Even Baron Massy was worried. He realized that putting Bernadette into an insane asylum might ignite a furor that could endanger his position, so he gave up the idea. After this, the civic authorities never dared to attack her directly.

Although the Baron was restrained from harassing Bernadette herself, he nevertheless commanded the police to place a barricade in front of the grotto and to arrest any pilgrims who approached.

Mr. Jacomet was very reluctant to carry out this order, even though he personally wanted to end the problem of policing the grotto. Yet, he did not wish to face the anger of the Lourdes merchants, who were doing a thriving trade serving the crowds flocking to the town. He also thought he might stir up a hornets' nest if he annoyed peaceful pilgrims by denying them access to the Lourdes Water. "After all, some of my own men believe in the miracles," he sighed.

In spite of these misgivings, he had to obey the Baron. He ordered his men to erect a palisade of planks around the holy spot. Crowds gathered outside this barricade, praying to Our Lady that it would soon come down. Many people, desperate for a cure for a loved one, broke through to get water from the spring. They were arrested by the police and fined five francs, a heavy penalty for a poor person.

CHAPTER SEVENTEEN
A GENTLE POWER

About a month after the barricade was erected, the Blessed Virgin appeared to Bernadette for the eighteenth and last time, on July 16, 1858. It was the Feast of Our Lady of Mount Carmel, the patroness of the stonecutters' guild of Lourdes. The Lady's appearance on this feast day was her farewell to Bernadette, who did not see her again in this world.

"She never looked so beautiful," Bernadette said. "She gazed at everyone lovingly and smiled her wonderful smile, but she did not speak."

Although the fence still barred pilgrims from entering the shrine, the Blessed Lady seemed just as close as before. Bernadette was confident that the Lady would cause the removal of the barricade. "We must not mind what men do," she said to her cousin, Jeanne Védère. "God permits it, so we must have patience. Those who put it up will have to take it down."

She was right. The Blessed Lady would display her gentle power. A tide of marvelous events would soon sweep away the wooden barrier and open the grotto to all.

A well-known journalist, Louis Veuillot, decided to visit Lourdes and see for himself what was drawing so many pilgrims. He was the editor of the daily

Catholic newspaper, *L'Univers,* and his opinions were respected by people at all levels of the church. In Lourdes, he met Mrs. Bruat, the wife of an Admiral of the French Navy. She was the governess of the Prince Imperial and one of the highest ranking ladies in the land. Mrs. Bruat arranged for the distinguished editor to visit Bernadette.

Providentially, Bernadette was able to receive Mr. Veuillot and Mrs. Bruat in the privacy of her own room at home, without disturbing her hard-working parents. This was possible because the Soubirous family had moved out of the dungeon and once more lived in a mill house.

The Bishop and Father Peyramale had found a new mill for François to manage. At last Bernadette's father could work at his trade and provide his family with a respectable home. In spite of enduring four years of destitution, followed by the intrusion of prying police and countless visitors, the Soubirous family had kept their self-respect and their faith.

During the visit with Bernadette, Mr. Veuillot listened attentively to her account of the apparitions. He was impressed with her honesty and captivated by her beautiful re-creation of the Lady's movements. After talking to Bernadette, the editor, along with Mrs. Bruat and other pilgrims, bypassed the wooden barrier, prayed at the grotto and collected some of the spring water—even though the guard warned them that this was against the law. The police arrested all the trespassers.

When the commissioner discovered the high position of Mr. Veuillot and Mrs. Bruat, he was dismayed. He knew that jailing them would get him in serious trouble, and soon ordered them released.

This incident dealt a heavy blow to the aspirations of those who wanted to ban entry to the grotto. More blows were coming.

Many bishops were impressed by the miracles, by the devotion of the Lourdes pilgrims, and by the conversion of unbelievers. All these signs pointed to a heavenly source for Bernadette's visions. To confirm the authenticity of the apparitions and the miracles, they urged Bishop Laurence of Tarbes to immediately authorize a church commission.

Bishop Laurence agreed to convene a Commission of Inquiry that would investigate and document the events at the site. He was fully aware that many false visionaries had arisen in the nineteen centuries of the Church's existence. He also knew that such claims could deceive even holy priests. As Lourdes was in his diocese, the Bishop was especially concerned because other young people suddenly began to claim that they saw visions at Massabielle. They said that they perceived frightening supernatural beings that gave them strange messages in the night. Shrieks and contortions of the visionaries accompanied these supposed visions. Their behavior was creating a disturbance.

The official Commission of Inquiry was set up in late July, 1858, a few weeks after the last apparition. The Commission included many experts. For four years, they conducted their examinations and talked to many witnesses. During this exhaustive process, bishops, priests, canon lawyers, medical doctors and others questioned Bernadette at length. She remained faithful to the Lady's message. She did not change her story an iota, repeating it in the same words time after time.

While she answered all questions with sincerity, often flavored with her delightful good humor, she sometimes protested, "But I have answered all your questions already. Why do you keep asking me the same things? Do you not believe me?"

The commissioners ignored the other young people that claimed to see visions; their activities soon ceased. The commissioners also treated the barricade as if it did not exist, and freely conducted their inquiry around the guards. Enforcement of the ban against entering the grotto became more and more lenient. The wooden planks were still up, but not for much longer.

CHAPTER EIGHTEEN

THE EMPEROR INTERVENES

Not far from Lourdes, at Biarritz, the Emperor of France, Louis Napoleon III, and his wife, the Empress Eugénie, were spending the summer at their villa along the shore of the Atlantic, on holiday from the court formalities of Paris. They took pleasure in the crashing surf and the ocean air. Their little son, Louis, the Prince Imperial, enjoyed flying his tiny kite and playing sailor with his small boats.

The family's joy faded, however, when little Louis caught a chill and lay on his bed, feverish and in pain. His doting mother hovered over him constantly. Her anxiety for her only child was making her beautiful face haggard and pale. It was no use for the doctor to assure her that the boy would soon be well. Nothing could console the frantic young mother, though the Emperor urged her not to worry.

"It is just some childhood ailment," he said soothingly. "The doctor would tell us if it were serious."

He looked at her with tenderness. He was deeply in love with his Spanish wife who had brought him the warmth of her generous and lively personality. Her gaiety enlivened his court. He was very proud of her. The high-born ladies of Europe copied her stylish hats and her elegant gowns. Her only fault, in his opinion, was that she took religion far too seriously.

"But, dear husband," she answered sorrowfully, "I have done everything the doctors ordered. I have kept his room warm. He has received his medicine regularly. He is fed only the lightest and purest food. But I am sure he is getting worse. And the doctors do not know what else to do. My poor Loulou." Tears filled her large brown eyes.

The Emperor felt helpless. He had surrounded the Empress with every luxury that money could offer, but who could buy the life of a child?

Just then Mrs. Bruat, the child's governess, entered. This was the same lady who, together with Mr. Veuillot, the editor of *L'Univers,* had been arrested at the grotto. Now this noble lady stood before the Emperor and Empress, holding a flask of the Lourdes Water.

After bowing deeply to the royal couple, Mrs. Bruat turned to the child's mother and asked, "Your Majesty, do you remember what I told you about Our Blessed Lady appearing at Lourdes?"

"Yes, yes," responded the Empress eagerly, "did you bring some of that miraculous water with you? Give it to me at once. If the doctors cannot heal my son, I hope and pray that the Virgin Mary may do so!"

The Emperor shrugged in pity at his wife's simple faith. He was Catholic and favorable to the Catholic cause, but he considered this talk of miracles to be simply ridiculous. Kissing his wife lightly on the cheek and bowing politely to Mrs. Bruat, he left the room.

The two women ardently prayed together. They then bathed the boy's fevered forehead with the water from Lourdes. They also coaxed him to sip a little.

The next morning the child sat up and demanded his favorite breakfast of croissants and hot chocolate. He was completely well and full of his usual high spirits. Overcome with joy, his mother gave thanks to God. She was resolute that orders be sent to open the grotto at Lourdes.

When the Empress sat with her husband for breakfast that morning, she talked with him about their son's recovery. She persuaded him to have the shrine reopened. She told him that she had vowed to do this if the prince was cured.

The Emperor smiled, delighted that his child was well and his wife had recovered her radiant beauty. Although he was well aware that many prominent people in France would be offended, he did not refuse the Empress her desire to keep her vow. That very day he sent orders to Baron Massy, the Prefect of Lourdes, to reopen the grotto immediately. Everyone who wished would be permitted to draw water from the spring.

The Emperor's orders were carried out with great pomp. On a sunny day on October 2, 1858, a grand ceremony took place at the grotto. The police in full dress uniform, to the beat of a large drum, accompanied Mayor Lacadé to the shrine.

With immense dignity, the mayor made the following proclamation, "On the orders of the Emperor, His Majesty Napoleon III, I solemnly declare that the public from now on may have free access to the grotto of Massabielle and to the waters of the spring. The barricade is to be taken down and not replaced."

The thousands of pilgrims gathered outside the barricade drowned out the drum with applause and cheers. Mayor Lacadé bowed to the assembly, as if he had personally arranged for this momentous act.

Captain Roques, the commanding officer of the military squadron at the castle, ordered his men to pull down the barrier. Splendid in his dress uniform and wearing his tufted military hat, he marched his soldiers to the front of the assembly. Captain Roques was present at one of the apparitions and had long believed in Bernadette's visions. His magnificent long mustache quivered with joy and pride as he unsheathed his sword and ordered his men to attack and destroy the wooden barricade.

The pilgrims rushed into the grotto with shouts of thanksgiving and praise. They helped the soldiers tear down the fence, and cleared a path to the grotto and the precious spring water.

The morning after the barricade was removed readers avidly discussed the article in the daily Catholic newspaper, *L'Univers*, headlined:

"EMPEROR ORDERS REOPENING OF SHRINE"

It was the first of many articles that kept Catholics informed of the events at Lourdes. The newspaper's editor, Louis Veuillot, was the renowned visitor who, along with Mrs. Bruat, the governess of the Prince Imperial, had been arrested for crossing the barricade at the grotto. His interview with Bernadette at that time convinced him of her complete sincerity. After the shrine reopened, Mr. Veuillot wrote persuasive editorials in his newspaper to encourage priests and teachers in France and surrounding countries to bring groups of pilgrims to the shrine.

The Catholic Church gave official approval for the public veneration of the Blessed Virgin at Lourdes after the Bishop's Commission of Inquiry completed its lengthy investigation, in January 1862. The Commission concluded that Bernadette was a true visionary, and that the Mother of God had actually appeared to her and was performing miracles through the spring water brought forth by Bernadette's hands.

Bishop Laurence then gave his authorization for a small church to be built at the site—the church that Our Lady had asked for. Money was raised and construction began in October 1862. Bernadette had the joy of seeing it finished and dedicated to the Immaculate Conception.

After the church was built, Pope Pius IX in Rome approved public worship at the shrine under the title of "Our Lady, the Immaculate Conception." This was a happy day for the Pope because he had proclaimed the dogma of the Immaculate Conception in 1854, fewer than four years before the apparitions. Many people had criticized the Pope for his action at the time, but now Our Lady herself had appeared, confirming the truth of his declaration.

Lourdes became a recognized pilgrimage site for devout Catholics from all over the world.

Chapter Nineteen

Boarding School

Everyone who visited the grotto also wanted to see Bernadette. They wanted to shake her hand, or hug her. They wanted to touch their rosary beads to hers. She received them all patiently, although she was worn out by the never-ending attention. Her cousin, Jeanne Védère, sympathized with her.

"Do you not get tired of standing here for hours?" she asked.

"The standing is not the worst, it is all these embraces," sighed Bernadette wearily. "Some foolish people even ask me to bless them as if I were a priest."

Bernadette was so deluged by visitors that she scarcely had time to participate in family meals and prayers. Sometimes, however, she had an hour of leisure in the afternoon. Then she and Toinette sat sewing in Bernadette's simple room, with its altar to the Blessed Lady always decorated with fresh flowers. There they prayed the rosary together and shared confidences and memories of old times. Bernadette was happy to become close to her sister again. She teased her about the young fellows who cast admiring glances toward her in church, "instead of saying their prayers."

Toinette had finished primary school and was growing up into a lovely and capable young lady. Her mama, worn out by poverty and distress, depended on her help with the house cleaning and cooking. Toinette was glad to learn the skills of housewifery because she hoped to have a home of her own when she got older.

Bernadette continued to attend the convent school as a day student. The nuns granted her this special privilege even though most students left the school after receiving their First Communion.

Eventually, however, she became so worn out and ill with the crush of visitors that Dr. Dozous stepped in to protect her. With Father Peyramale, he arranged to send her to Cauterets, a mountain resort that was well-known for its hot springs. There she enjoyed some privacy and peace. Basking in the sunshine of the bathing resort, Bernadette lived like an ordinary tourist. She went to the hot baths each day and gladly joined in conversation with the other tourists. Yet, she was most content when she was alone.

Sometimes she climbed along a mountain trail, enjoying the sight of cascading streams and strange rock formations. From lofty heights Bernadette gazed at what has been called "the most beautiful scenery in the world." In enclaves strewn with delicate mountain flowers, she marveled at God's tiny masterpieces.

She spent most of her solitude praying the rosary and recalling every word, every gesture and every smile of the Blessed Lady. Each day she repeated the special prayer the Lady had given her, and hugged to her heart the secrets the Lady had revealed, the personal secrets that she never told anyone.

Bernadette returned to Lourdes after a few weeks, refreshed in body and spirit. She braced herself to meet with thousands of pilgrims again—but she was in for a happy surprise.

Father Peyramale had been busy while she was away. For two years, the crowds had enjoyed almost unlimited access to Bernadette. Her pastor was concerned about her health. He and other authorities in the Church also feared that she could become conceited if adoring pilgrims continued to besiege her. The priest convinced the Sisters of Charity and Christian Instruction at the convent school to take Bernadette as a boarding student. This way the nuns could protect her from the adulation and exhausting demands of the pilgrims. As she was a boarder, visitors outside of her own family could not see her, with a few exceptions, including bishops and some priests.

To shield Bernadette from the crowds, two nuns accompanied her when she went to pray at the grotto. She could visit her family only on Sundays. To protect her privacy, Mother Superior warned the sisters and the other students not to bother her with questions. Although the nuns were secretly in awe of the little visionary who had seen the Blessed Virgin, they treated her just as they did every other student, with kindness and firmness. Bernadette made no outward display of her deep spiritual life. She generally behaved like the other students, except that she was more lively and full of pranks than most.

One day Bernadette passed her box of snuff, which she took for her asthma, around the classroom. Soon all the girls were sneezing and giggling. In the confusion, the teacher thought the whole class had come down with colds. Then she caught the mischief-maker. It was difficult for the teacher to be severe, but she gave Bernadette a suitable penalty.

Another time, Bernadette and her playful friend, Julie Garros, hatched a plot to raid the nuns' strawberry patch. Bernadette threw her shoe out of the window into the garden. Julie then had to go out to rescue it. She brought it back full of strawberries. Although the penalty for this trick was staying in the classroom at recreation time, the culprits agreed it was worth it; the berries were delicious.

The nuns insisted on complete obedience from their students, but Bernadette was stubborn. One of the hardest battles of wills was over her Sunday dress.

The convent school had a simple dress code. All the students wore a plain long skirt, a long-sleeved blouse and a shawl over their shoulders, crossed and pinned in front. The girls selected colors, hairstyles and ornaments according to their own taste.

On Sundays, the students were expected to wear an attractive but modest dress to Mass at the parish church of St. Peter. Because Bernadette's family was too poor to buy her such a dress, the sewing mistress of the school made one for her. The lovely pale blue dress was embroidered with lilies and trimmed with hand-crocheted lace. Bernadette was thrilled. Until then, she had never owned a pretty dress.

"You mean it is my very own?" she exclaimed, giving a huge grateful hug to the sewing mistress.

Bernadette planned to wear it on Sunday and then hurry to the mill house after Mass to display it to her mama and papa. How pleased they would be to see their daughter so beautifully dressed. Bernadette knew her mama had been ashamed that she could only provide her daughters with shabby clothes.

To Bernadette's immense frustration, the nuns refused to allow her to wear her beautiful dress on her visit to her family. After Mass, she was told to return directly to the convent and remove the dress, lest she get it dirty. Bernadette pleaded for permission to show it to her parents first. The nun in charge that day was a highborn lady that had given up all her lovely clothes and now wore only her plain black habit. She did not understand the desires of a poor girl who had never before owned any nice-looking clothes.

"But it is my own dress," Bernadette protested vehemently. "The sewing mistress said so. I will not take it off until Mama and Papa have seen it."

Greatly displeased by this defiance, the nun sent Bernadette to her room until she changed. The girl sat on her bed and sobbed. She was suddenly homesick and longed to feel her mama's comforting arms around her. What did she care if she missed dinner?

Finally, a young nun came into Bernadette's room. She was understanding and consoled the forlorn student. Very gently, she gave her youthful charge a lecture on humility and obedience. It was a bad example to the whole school when one pupil refused to obey, the nun explained. She coaxed Bernadette to take off the dress and get ready for dinner.

The very next Sunday, however, the nuns relented and allowed Bernadette to visit her parents wearing her new dress.

In the atmosphere of kindness and peace in the convent school, Bernadette advanced quickly in her studies. With good food and plenty of recreation, she became healthier. She learned to read hard books and to write in the artistic and elegant handwriting of the time. She learned to speak proper French, to do arithmetic, to embroider and even to draw. Best of all she attended Mass every day at the convent chapel and was allowed to receive Communion as often as once a week—a rare privilege in those days. Her four years as a student passed happily. When she graduated at the age of eighteen years, she was allowed to remain at the convent as a working guest.

CHAPTER TWENTY

BERNADETTE LEAVES LOURDES FOREVER

One Friday afternoon, Bernadette was scraping carrots in a corner of the large kitchen in the convent. This was one of her daily jobs as a working guest of the nuns. Suddenly the bell rang to call her to the parlor. She quickly removed her large white apron and left the vegetables to the cook.

Bernadette entered the nuns' parlor with some awe. This elegant room, furnished with velvet-covered chairs and highly polished tables, was used only on formal occasions. There she was greeted by an exalted visitor, Bishop Forcade of Nevers. The kindly prelate invited Bernadette to sit in one of the chairs drawn up to a small table. She curtsied to him, kissed the ring on his extended hand, and sat facing him with poised expectancy.

"What do you want to do with your life, Bernadette?" he asked.

"I am happy to stay here with the sisters who have been so kind to me," she answered.

"Would you like to become one of the Sisters of Charity like the nuns here?"

Bernadette was overjoyed. This would be an answer to her prayers and dreams—but she had to be sure.

"Perhaps they will not take me," she replied. "After all, I am good for nothing. I have bad health and no dowry. Why should they accept me into their order?"

The Bishop assured her that the nuns would be pleased to have her join their community. Or, she could choose among three other orders of nuns who had offered to accept her, if she preferred. Bernadette chose to join the Sisters of Charity and Christian Instruction, the nuns who had given her free schooling and a happy life as a student.

This was a wonderful, but difficult, move for Bernadette. She was twenty-two years old, and had always lived among people who had known her from birth. Now she was about to leave her home and family forever, and travel to the motherhouse of the Sisters of Charity, in the distant town of Nevers, hundreds of miles northeast of Lourdes.

Bernadette never again returned to Lourdes or the place where she had seen the Blessed Lady. "I glimpsed heaven here," she said, weeping, when she visited the grotto on the day before she left.

Three nuns and another postulant accompanied Bernadette on her train ride from Lourdes to Nevers. It was a long journey from the sunny foothills of the Pyrenees Mountains in southern France to the misty valley of the placid Loire River. It was a long journey indeed from the close companionship of family and friends to the formality and austerity of the cloister.

Upon entering the massive gate to the courtyard of St. Gildard's, the motherhouse of the Sisters of Charity, Bernadette looked up at the large cross above the gate. It was shining in the moonlight. She gazed thoughtfully at the Heart of Jesus encircled by a crown of thorns.

"Yes," she said to Jesus, silently accepting the crosses and the crown of thorns that she knew would accompany life in her new home.

The convent was quiet when the weary travelers arrived. Bernadette observed the dim, spacious gardens and large, noble buildings that cast long shadows in the moonlight. Stepping across the threshold into the main foyer, she was grateful to be wearing the new dress and shoes her aunt had bought for her. Her wooden shoes and Pyrenean kerchief would have been out of place in the dignified reception hall.

Mother Imbert was awake to receive them. The Mother Superior welcomed Bernadette with cool formality. Her blue eyes seemed to penetrate deep into the young woman's soul, even as she explained convent life to her and asked about her family and about her expectations of life at the convent. Bernadette answered the questions simply, with her usual quiet confidence.

The Superior conducted Bernadette down a long hall to the dormitory where a bed had been prepared for her. One nun silently glided past them, apparently intent on some duty, but at the same time stealing a glance at this famous newcomer. Everyone in the convent was seething with excitement about having

Bernadette join them. They were all curious to see the young woman who had seen the Blessed Virgin.

Before leaving her, Mother Imbert said, "The convent is not a prison, Bernadette. If you should desire to leave, you have only to let me know."

The next day Bernadette began to wear the garb of a "little bonnet," as the postulants were called. They dressed in black robes with white collars, their youthful faces framed in lace-trimmed bonnets. Over the next few years, they would learn how to properly conduct themselves as nuns, before taking their final vows as professed sisters.

Bernadette's name in religious life was Sister Marie-Bernarde, the same as her Baptismal name. Especially in those early days, she felt the full force of her sacrifice in becoming a nun. The tears she held back when she was among the others burst from the depths of her soul during the night. In the formality of the bell that summoned them to meals, the silence, and the gardens enclosed by stone walls, the young postulant could foresee the next years of her life.

Mother Imbert understood the new arrival's terrible homesickness, and took her for short outings, talking to her about the glory of a life dedicated to God. Gradually, Bernadette's feelings of loneliness and grief subsided.

Despite her bouts of asthma, she found joy in her new life. Yet, God allowed a painful thorn to remain—the nun in charge of the "little bonnets" treated her with scorn. This mistress of novices, Mother Marie Thérèse Vazous, did not believe that Bernadette had seen a heavenly vision. "If you want to prove to me that you saw the Blessed Virgin, you must tell me the secrets she told you," insisted Mother Vazous.

"But I cannot do that, Mother," Bernadette replied. "If I told you, they would no longer be secret, would they?"

Mother Vazous' mouth set in a thin line, showing her vexation. She could not fathom why the Blessed Virgin would appear to such a stupid and unrefined person. For the next eleven years, as long as she remained at the Nevers convent, Mother Vazous took every opportunity to make cutting remarks, to rebuff, reprove and silence the younger nun.

"It is necessary to teach Sister Marie-Bernarde humility so that she will not become proud of the attention she has received in the world," Mother Vazous explained to the other novices.

Many years later, a nun from another convent had a conversation with Bernadette. She noted that, when Mother Vazous passed near them, Bernadette hid her face behind her mending and exclaimed softly, "Oh, how I fear her."

The other sisters felt sorry for their companion as they witnessed her enduring daily rebukes and ridicule. They came to love her exuberance and sense of fun. Yet, imitating their superior, they generally kept their warm feelings to themselves and showed her scant affection. Sister Vareillaud, who was a novice with Bernadette and saw how contemptuously she was treated, admitted later that she often thought, "How lucky I am not to be Bernadette!"

Bernadette endured the "martyrdom of the heart" caused by these incessant humiliations without a single complaint.

Shortly after she entered the convent, Bernadette was told to address an assembly of all the nuns about the apparitions of the Blessed Virgin. It was the only time she was asked to describe her experience to the other sisters.

Her story of seeing the beautiful Lady, dressed in blue and white with yellow roses on her feet, captivated her audience. They watched, spellbound, as she showed them the big, slow Sign of the Cross the Lady had taught her; how she had gestured and moved; what she had said (except for the secrets and her special prayer); and above all, how her smile radiated love.

When Bernadette finished speaking, her audience clapped excitedly, but Mother Vazous cut them off. "That will be all," she said abruptly, unable to hide her dislike of the visionary and her disbelief in the story of the apparitions.

To the other novices, she added, "Now that you have heard Sister Marie-Bernarde's story, I forbid you to ask her any more questions. From now on, no one will discuss these events." The nuns were dismissed. Perhaps they talked about this wondrous story quietly when they walked in the spacious gardens, far from Mother Vazous' sharp ears, but they did not talk about the apparitions with the visionary herself.

Bernadette loved to spend time in the chapel praying to Jesus in the Blessed Sacrament, and to read and meditate in the park-like gardens. She especially treasured one corner of the garden, where a statue of Our Lady of the Waters was set in a rocky niche. It was a simple statue with its arms held out graciously. It was here that the lonely nun poured out her sorrows and experienced her mystic joys.

"Of all the statues I have seen, it is the most like the beautiful Lady I saw at the grotto," she said.

Bernadette's favorite place to work was the infirmary of the convent, where she skillfully cared for the sick nuns and dispensed their medicine as the doctor ordered. She was fond of the rows of white-covered beds, the cupboards for medical supplies, and the altar to the Blessed Lady. Like her mother, Louise, Bernadette was "half-doctor" by nature.

Back in their Lourdes home, François and Louise Soubirous had to work at the mill every day except Sundays, so they could not make the long journey to visit their daughter at the convent in Nevers. Indeed, Bernadette did not see her parents again in this life. Louise died just a few months after Bernadette left Lourdes. The postulant was so overcome with grief when she received the news of her mother's death that she fainted.

Even without the help of his wife, François continued to run the mill until his own death five years later. He received all visitors with courteous patience, in thanksgiving for the favors that the Blessed Virgin had granted to his child.

Not many visitors were allowed to see Bernadette, except for her relatives, who rarely visited, and bishops and priests. Others were admitted only in desperate cases, to plead for her prayers.

On one such occasion, a mother came to the convent with her baby boy, who was covered with incurable sores. Bernadette carried the sick child around the garden a few times. By the time she brought him back and laid him in his mother's arms, he was completely healed.

On another occasion, a little girl visitor asked, "Was the Lady really so lovely?"

"Ah," sighed Bernadette, "she was so beautiful that to see her again one would gladly die."

A few years after she entered the convent, the doctor discovered that Bernadette had tuberculosis of the bone. This caused her intense pain. In spite of her suffering, the industrious little nun always did her work well, when she was able. She remained lively and funny, and made the other sisters laugh with her droll imitations.

Eventually, disease overcame Bernadette's feeble body. She had frequent attacks of asthma; once she almost died of pneumonia. As the tuberculosis worsened, she became an invalid. She then spent long hours on her bed in the infirmary, in relentless pain, shielded from drafts by white curtains.

"My bed is my little chapel," she said with good-humored courage. She pinned holy images onto the curtains around her bed, thinking, "I can still pray if I can do nothing else."

Even in her sick bed, she tried to keep busy. She painted pictures of a heart surrounded by thorns on little cards that she sent to the people who corresponded with her.

"They can't say I am heartless," she joked.

In her final months, it was evident to all that she was dying—though she often dragged herself to the chapel to hear Mass and receive Holy Communion. When her death was imminent, Bishop Forcade of Nevers, who had first suggested that she become a nun, came to the convent to give her the Last Rites of the Church, the anointing and blessings that would help prepare her for her final journey to life in the next world.

"You are being asked to make a great sacrifice, the sacrifice of your life," he said with gentle respect.

"That is no sacrifice," Bernadette whispered, amazed that he did not know how she longed to see her Blessed Mother again.

Father Peyramale, Bernadette's former pastor, traveled all the way from Lourdes to visit her. He told her of the great new basilica being built on the crest of Massabielle in honor of the Immaculate Conception. He told her of the thousands of people being healed and turning back to God. He told her of the candlelight processions in the evenings.

Bernadette was comforted in her final sufferings, knowing that the Blessed Lady's requests continued to be fulfilled.

CHAPTER TWENTY-ONE

IN BLESSED REPOSE

Bernadette died at the Convent of St. Gildard in Nevers, in 1879, at thirty-five years of age. Her spiritual sisters, the nuns at Nevers, had come to love her dearly. Even Mother Vazous' heart eventually softened, although not until many years later.

Although Bernadette endured so much pain while she lived, her frail body miraculously did not decay after she died. It was preserved incorrupt. In death, Bernadette's body became more beautiful than when she was alive; all signs of her suffering disappeared, leaving her face gentle and peaceful.

To this day, more than 150 years after her death, pilgrims visit St. Gildard's Convent in Nevers to view Bernadette's body where it rests in a glass casket trimmed with gold. A rosary is in her hands and she seems to be sleeping, as if waiting for her resurrection on the last day when Jesus comes in glory.

Decades after Bernadette's death, the universal Church officially recognized her extraordinary sanctity. In a splendid ceremony at the Vatican in Rome, on the Feast of the Immaculate Conception, December 8, 1933, Pope Pius XI declared that Bernadette is a saint in heaven—allowing her to be venerated in the sacred liturgy. This joyous event was the final fruit of the miracles at Lourdes and the long investigation of Bernadette begun by Bishop Laurence of Tarbes in 1858.

Although many cardinals and other dignitaries of the Catholic Church attended the service, the only person at the canonization ceremony that had known Bernadette during her childhood was a 77-year-old man from Lourdes, Justin Bouhouhorts. He had been the first to be healed at the grotto, for he was the dying baby whose distraught mother prayed and plunged him into the Lourdes Spring.

The Blessed Lady's serene and loving spirit still reigns over Lourdes; many of the millions of pilgrims that visit the shrine each year receive some favor from her. Invalids in wheelchairs in front of the grotto are sometimes cured as the priest blesses them with the Sacred Host. Some are healed on the way home from Lourdes. Suzanne Gestas, who was seriously ill with tubercular peritonitis, was cured on the train after leaving Lourdes. A few that went to Lourdes with no faith have been cured. Gabriel Gargam, who had not practiced his religion for fifteen years and refused to see a priest during twenty months of hospitalization, was healed both physically and spiritually.

A Medical Bureau was established at Lourdes in 1885. Its staff and physicians continue to examine claimed healings "with conscientious exactitude." They have found many cures to be "beyond the power of nature or science."

In official documents, the Immaculate Conception's beloved little messenger is called Saint Marie-

Bernarde, her Baptismal and religious name. But most know her simply as Saint Bernadette, the fourteen-year-old girl who saw the Queen of Heaven in the grotto at Lourdes in 1858; the girl who fearlessly announced the Blessed Lady's name, request for a chapel, and messages of love, prayer and penance to the whole world.

Important Dates in Bernadette's Life

January 7, 1844—Bernadette Soubirous born in the Boly Mill at Lourdes.

June, 1854—Soubirous family leaves Boly Mill.

February 11 to July 16, 1858—The Blessed Virgin Mary appears eighteen times to Bernadette at the grotto of Massabielle.

June 8, 1858—Solemn municipal decree closes access to the grotto and its spring. Trespassers arrested and fined.

July 28, 1858—Bishop Laurence of Tarbes and Lourdes appoints a Commission of Inquiry into the apparitions.

October 2, 1858—Emperor Napoleon III orders reopening of the grotto.

January 18, 1862—Based on the four-year investigation by the Commission of Inquiry, the Bishop of Tarbes recognizes the apparitions as authentic in the eyes of the church.

July 4, 1866—Bernadette leaves Lourdes for the convent in Nevers.

July 29, 1866—Bernadette receives the religious habit of the Congregation of the Sisters of Charity of Nevers and is given the name, Sister Marie-Bernarde.

December, 1866—Bernadette's mother dies at the age of 41.

March 4, 1871—Bernadette's father dies at the age of 64.

April 16, 1879—Bernadette dies at the age of 35.

June 14, 1925 —Bernadette beatified.

December 8, 1933—Bernadette canonized a saint by Pope Pius XI.

About the Author

At 73 years of age, Letitia "Lettie" Morse began writing the story of St. Bernadette. After two years, she completed the manuscript. After fourteen years, at the age of 88, she had the joy of seeing her book published in 2008, the 150th anniversary year of the apparitions.

Lettie was born Violet Mary Cortens in Winnipeg, Canada, in 1920. The name Letitia was added later by her godmother. She and her husband, Allan, live in Ottawa, Canada. They have eight children, twenty-five grandchildren and fourteen great-grandchildren.

In 1966, Lettie and her husband made a pilgrimage to Lourdes with their daughter, Diane, who has Down Syndrome. During that visit, Allan and Lettie witnessed two healings in their daughter. She was cured of chronic colds when she bathed in the Lourdes water, and she received the gift of compassion for Our Savior's sufferings while praying the life-sized outdoor Stations of the Cross at the shrine.

On this visit, however, Lettie did not learn much about Bernadette; she only noticed her statue standing alone in the background of the shrine. Years later, during her research for this book, the author gained a deep affection and admiration for Bernadette's liveliness, sense of humor, integrity and courage.

Throughout her long life, the author has observed the cultural and spiritual havoc wrought by some of the events and changes of the past century. More than ever, she believes, people need meaning in their lives, and a more fervent faith. Her prayer is that this life of St. Bernadette of Lourdes, Our Lady's little messenger, will inspire hope and new courage in each reader.

APPENDIX C

ACKNOWLEDGMENTS

I am grateful to the many people that supported my work on this book and helped bring it to publication.

My husband, Allan Morse, read each chapter as it was written and sustained me with his editorial skill and enthusiasm.

My daughter, Dr. Jean Morse-Chevrier, and her husband, Dr. Jacques Chevrier, provided valuable technical help, made numerous phone calls and wrote letters to aid with the publication. My children and other family members, especially Vincent Chevrier, Zach Aysan, Teresa Aysan, Mary Jo McLeod, and Trudi Cortens, read the book and gave much-valued encouragement and advice. Of these, my granddaughter, Evelyne Chevrier (now Suomela), purchased literature on St. Bernadette for me when she was in Lourdes on pilgrimage.

Thanks to the French Embassy in Ottawa, I received brochures on the beautiful Pyrenees region.

Members of the Children's Literature Institute in West Redding, Connecticut, helped me acquire the basic techniques of writing for publication. In particular I appreciate Terri Martini who critiqued each chapter and gave me the benefit of her experience on how to improve the writing in specific detail. Her unflagging encouragement was instrumental in my successful completion of the book.

Michael O'Brien, artist and the bestselling author of *Strangers and Sojourners* and *Elijah*, published my first stories for children in his (then) magazine, *Nazareth*. He strongly encouraged me to continue to write.

The Ave Maria prayer group of Ottawa not only prayed for God's blessings on the writing, but some of them also read the manuscript and made helpful suggestions. Among these I particularly appreciate the encouragement of my friend, Rita Tevlin (now Cullen), during the early stages.

Editors at Ignatius Press, Our Sunday Visitor Press, and St. Mary's Press wrote encouraging letters, even though they were unable to publish this book. Also I much appreciate François Vayne, Director of Communications at the shrine in Lourdes, France, who first expressed interest in publishing the book.

My spiritual director during the writing process was Father Francis Martin, scripture scholar and author, who presently chairs Catholic/Jewish theological studies of the John Paul II Cultural Center in Washington, D.C. He urged me to send my writing to publishers.

Mary Lynn Hanley (now Cihak) has been the "godmother" of the book. She first suggested I write the story of St. Bernadette for children, and gave invaluable support and editorial comments. She and her husband, Dr. Robert Cihak, through their publishing company, Bienna Books, based in the Seattle,

Washington area, have now become its editors and publishers. I owe them a great debt of gratitude for dedicating many hours of work; for careful research and editing; for their choices of design, layout and the artistic cover; and most of all for overcoming obstacles with unflagging enthusiasm over many months. They have been co-creators of the book, rather than merely business partners.

Brother Lawrence Lew, O.P., of the Dominican community of Blackfriars in Oxford, England, kindly allowed us to use his beautiful photos of the stained glass windows in the basilica at Lourdes as a basis for the cover design. He has continued to support our efforts through his interest and prayers.

Brian Gage Design of Vancouver, Washington, designed the book cover. I appreciate the creative talent and care of the graphic designers, Calvin Carl, Brian Gage and Ryan Schroeder, and the illustrator, Parker Fitzgerald. Special thanks to Michael Perry for the interior layout and for his valuable help in working with the printer, Lightning Source.

Finally I would like to thank Brian Suomela for help with software, and Gerry Gauvreau for his many hours of volunteer work on my computer.

This book is dedicated to St. Bernadette and to the Immaculate Heart of Mary. My debt to them is incalculable. In writing it, I came to know them more deeply and to feel their presence guiding me. Without their spiritual support, I am sure this book would never have been written or published.

Printed in the United States
129685LV00001B/57/P

9 780981 507507